CREDIT SECRETS

2 Books in 1

The complete guide to check and repair a negative Credit Score to take full control of your credit and finances. Inside 609 template letters.

ANDREW BENNET

Credit Score

STEP 1

STEP 2

STEP 3

Introduction

FICO and Vantage Score both indicate that about two-thirds of Americans have a rating of good or better. This statistic shows promise for people who are attempting to build credit. It is not that difficult to do if you are careful with how you use your available credit.

Mortgage providers (the companies providing credit for home loans) indicate that even people with low credit scores can apply for home loans. The biggest difference is that you may not get favourable terms and good interest rates if your credit score is poor. Many lending institutions require a minimum down payment of 10% and additional security if your credit score is below 580. In contrast, a credit score higher than 580 only necessitates a 3.5% down payment. This example clearly shows why a good credit score is better for people.

How Many Types of Credit Scores Are There?

Businesses have credit scores just like individuals, but the ratings work in a slightly different manner. You may be operating a business and need to take out a loan or purchase a vehicle on finance for company purposes. The major difference lies in the actual credit scores: business credit scores fall within a range of zero to 100. Similar rules still apply and the closer your business is to a score of 100, the better it will be for your credit applications.

The Experian score is broken down into more segments: high-risk businesses score 1 to 10; medium to high-risk score 11 – 25; medium risk is obtained by businesses with a score of 26 to 50. The segments then become slightly larger. Businesses scoring between 51 and 75 pose a low to medium risk for lenders, and the lowest risk is when a business has a score of 76 to 100.

Equifax works slightly differently. They have one rating system for payment history and another for the likelihood that your business will fail. Instead of describing the scores in terms of risk, Equifax gives a ranking based on how you pay or how late your payment is to your creditors. Paying your creditors as agreed gives a score of 90 – 100; if you pay in the 30 days following the due date then your score is 80 – 89. A score of 60 – 79 is attributed for payment 31 to 60 days after the due date. Paying creditors 61 to 90 days late will result in a 40 – 59 credit score; while a score of 20 – 39 is given for payment between days 91 and 120.

Some lenders use an Application Score between 100 and 990, and Credit Optics Score by ID Analytics Inc. between 1 and 999.

Several websites (Trans Union, Equifax, Credit Karma, Credit Sesame etc.) offer different credit scores to consumers but are not used by lenders. Innovis, ChexSystems and PRBC are other companies that produce credit scores used by some lenders.

Here's really all you need to know. You have a Vantage Score from each of the bureaus. They use the exact same formula because they all joined forces to create the formula. You would have the exact same Vantage Score from each bureau if you had the same information in each bureau. Although it's highly unlikely you have the same information in all the bureaus. The Vantage Score is used by only 10% of lenders.

You also a FICO score from each bureau. Used by 90% of credit lenders. This score would also be the same for each bureau if you had the same information in each bureau. This again is highly unlikely.

You also have Industry Specific FICO Scores from each of the bureaus. Credit Cards, Auto Industry, Installment Loan, Personal Finance and finally Mortgage.

Three Major Credit Bureaus, Three Credit Scores, Two Models Rating Agencies

There are 3 main Credit Bureaus that crunch the numbers and create a credit score that defines your score: Trans Union, Equifax, and Experian (There are in fact other companies, smaller ones, but these are the 3 we will focus on). Each Credit Bureau looks at different aspects of your financial profile. What this means is that, for example, Experian will take a heavy consideration on late credit card payments, but Equifax may not focus so much on that.What is Credit Score

What affects Your Credit Score

The three main credit bureaus calculate your FICO score when assigning you a credit score. FICO scores are made up of the five key factors of "payment history, current level of indebtedness, types of credit used, length of credit history, and new credit accounts" (Hayes, 2019, para. 1) to calculate your score. Since the biggest companies focus on these factors, bringing up your credit score most commonly involves addressing these areas and making changes where necessary to score better in each field. While all five factors contribute to your overall score, your payment history and your current level of debt are weighted the heaviest, so let's look at these first.

Past Payment History

It supplies information about all of your previous debt payments, including how quickly you paid them off, whether you met all payment due dates on time, if you incurred any late fees, and if you repeatedly missed payments and ended up in collections. This score is calculated using all forms of repayment, which is everything from home mortgages to credit cards to student loan debt. It does not include loans given to you by friends and family, as these loans are not reported to credit bureaus, and typically the only thing you risk by not paying them back in a timely manner is incurring your friends' wrath.

Though it is called a payment history, this does not mean that a few missteps will permanently keep you from a higher credit score. Debts that go to collections and declaring bankruptcies can impact your credit score severely when they occur, but if you proceed to build up many on-time payments and demonstrate that you have changed the way you handle your finances, it can help to balance these less positive events out and even outweigh them.

Payment history gives lenders the best picture of what you are like as a debtor and how much of a risk you would be should they approve you. The best way to ensure you have a healthy credit score is to make sure your payment history is in order, which you can achieve by always making at least the minimum payments on time and trying not to use the maximum amount of credit granted to you.

Total Amount of Debt

Your level of debt makes up 30 percent of a FICO credit score, making it nearly as influential as your payment history. Having too many outstanding debts can make creditors unwilling to give you a new one, as they are uncertain whether or not you can handle so much debt at a time. For example, if you already owe $80,000 in student loans, it can be hard to get approved for a mortgage on a $300,000 house, as it would saddle you with a very high amount of debt altogether. The higher your total debt, the less likely you are to be able to pay it off, which can make lenders uncertain. Credit balances that are maxed out or over the available limit really hurt your score in this category.

Keep in mind that your current income level is not part of your credit score, so even if you make much more than your current debts, they can still harm your score. Say you make $150,000 a year, but you have $30,000 in unpaid credit card debt. You could probably afford to pay a great deal of it, but if you merely make the minimum payment each month, the remainder still counts as outstanding debt. If you can make payments and reduce your debts, you should do so whenever possible.

Length of Credit History

It makes up 15 percent of your FICO credit score, so it is relatively important, but not a game changer. Younger people often have trouble with this aspect, as many do not consider credit to be a necessity until they encounter a credit roadblock that gets in the way of a purchase.

This is why it is always a good idea to start looking at your credit as early as possible.

Having a longer credit history provides a pattern of behaviour that showcases a more complete picture of your financial habits. On the other hand, a brief period of financial turmoil is more easily remedied in a longer credit history of making payments on time. This is true for both individual credit lines and your credit history as a whole.

Types of Credit

Credit is broken down into three main types known as revolving credit, instalment credit, and open credit. Each of these types deals with different sources of loans. Your mix of these different credit types accounts for 10 percent of your FICO credit score. While it is far from the most important factor, having a good balance of credit types can still bring your score up a few points. To do so, you must know what each category of credit means.

The first type, **revolving credit**, is commonly associated with credit cards and home equity loans. It does not require you to make a fixed number of payments, but you are required to pay a minimum balance based on how much debt you have every term, usually monthly. Revolving credit also typically charges interest on unpaid debt, and usually sets a credit limit on how much you can borrow at a time. Aside from your credit limit and monthly payments, revolving credit is relatively unstructured, and allows you to pay off your debts at your own leisure provided you continue to make at least the minimum payment.

Installment credit usually deals with larger loans that you take out for big life events. These can be student loans, auto loans, mortgages, personal loans, or many other kinds. Repayment is much more structured than with revolving credit. Payments are regularly scheduled and require a fixed amount that does not fluctuate under normal circumstances, though certain factors like changes to the terms of your loan or attempts to refinance can alter the amount you are required to pay each period. Most forms of instalment credit will take a while to pay off in full, unlike revolving credit, which tends to be much more manageable to pay all at once.

Generally, charge cards and any other forms of open credit require you to pay the entire balance at the end of a payment period, while credit cards usually have a minimum payment that does not account for the entire bill. Open credit typically does not have a spending limit either.

Ideally, you should have at least two different kinds of credit rather than having all your credit be the same type. However, it is not worth opening new accounts just to achieve this goal, as your credit diversity accounts for a low portion of your score and opening too many accounts can negatively impact your credit, negating any positive effects.

Amount of New Credit

This is a less well-known factor, but the number of new credit lines you open within the last year can impact your score. Oftentimes, especially for younger people and those newer to credit, you will be tempted to open multiple different accounts to start building your credit, but opening too many in a short period can actually harm it. You should try to keep your number of new accounts to just one or two per year if you can, as this will minimize the impact on your score.

Opening new lines of credit can hurt your score because each new line of credit you apply for must check your credit score. Additionally, a new line of credit lowers your length of credit history, a score factor, so you will want to avoid making an unreasonable number of new accounts in a year.

Chapter 1. What is Credit Report

A credit report is a comprehensive account of your financial history. Credit bureaus begin gathering information about you the moment you apply for a credit card, take out a loan, or open a utility account, and use that information to generate a credit report. Lenders will then use this report, along with the other details you provide, to assess your creditworthiness.

Where to find Your Credit Report

The Fair Credit Reporting Act (FCRA) requires credit bureaus to provide customers with a free copy of their credit report once a year. Consumers are therefore entitled to a free credit report if a corporation takes adverse action against them under federal law. Denial of jobs, insurance, or credit, as well as notices of collections or judgments, are examples of adverse action. The customer must, however, request the report within 60 days of the occurrence of the adverse action. You'll still be eligible to get a free credit check if you're on welfare or unemployment, or if you've been the victim of identity fraud.

What Is The Best Way To Get A Free Credit Report?

If you're reading this from anywhere else in the country, I'm afraid you'll have to look elsewhere. It could be your government position, a credit officer, or something else. However, if you're curious how to do it in the United States, it's all set out here.

You should keep in mind that if you check a similar site rather than this one, you may be fined or, worse, you may be playing into a fraudster's trap. Select your desired credit report after filling out your personal details (whether Equifax, Experian, or Trans union). On the next screen, you must confirm your identity by answering a few questions about your credit history. After that, the credit report appears on the computer. You can either print or return to display the document. Right on the money. If this does not work, call 1-877-322-8228 and follow the same steps over the internet. You'll have to wait a couple of weeks, if not longer, to get your credit report.

The FICO Scoring Model

Because of its long track record, FICO has the distinction of being the most accurate scoring model. The Fair Isaac Company started calculating these scores in 1989. They've updated the algorithms many times over the last three decades to account for changing factors and ensure that they continue to deliver consistent credit scores.

As previously mentioned, the conventional FICO score model will give you a score between 300 and 850. A score of less than 600 is considered low. It is considered outstanding if your score is greater than 740.

Between 600 and 740, credit worthiness varies from average to above average.

FICO launched its FICO 9 scoring model in 2014. The biggest change in this model was to downplay the significance of unpaid medical bills. The rationale behind this is that unpaid medical debts are not true financial health indicators.

You could be waiting for insurance to cover a medical bill, or you could be completely unaware that a medical bill has been sent to a collection agency. For certain individuals, this significant improvement resulted in a 25-point rise in their credit score.

Other amendments made in 2017 made it illegal for collectors to record late medical debts that were not even 180 days past due. The three credit reporting bureaus have removed all details on civil judgments and tax lien reports from their archives in 2017. According to FICO, this improved the scores of around 6% of customers.

FICO 8 (which the company created in 2009) was the standard credit score version until FICO 9. The FICO 8 score is now the most widely used in the lending industry. The distinguishing features of FICO 8 were that it penalized you for spending near your total credit limit per month and granted you clemency if you had only one 30-day late payment.

It's worth noting that when FICO updates its scoring models, lenders have the option of keeping their current version or upgrading. Since upgrading to the new model is so costly, FICO 8 has remained the strong favorite. Also FICO 5 models are still used by some lenders.

During the application process, you can inquire about the model your lender is using.

In most cases, FICO scores do not change substantially in the short term. The only exception is if you start missing payments or have charge-offs or defaults on your account. FICO scores aren't available to all. If you don't have credit, you'll be classified as "credit invisible," according to experts.

To get a FICO ranking, you must have six months of payments recorded to the credit bureaus.

You've heard it before: you need a high FICO score to get this kind of credit, this kind of interest rate, and this kind of privilege. The single most important aspect that stands between you and almost everything you want is your FICO ranking.

Although many people are aware of the effect of their FICO score on their credit, few could explain what it is or how it is calculated if asked. Given the power this number wields over so many people, it's surprising that more people don't inquire as to what it is or what they can do about it. They actually embrace the fact that this number wields so much influence over their lives.

A person has many credit scores; however, the FICO Score is the most well-known and is used by the majority of lenders. Understanding the factors that influence how it is measured will help you stay informed about the acts that have a positive or negative impact on your ranking. You can make a big impact on your score by concentrating on the major factors mentioned below that can positively affect it.

Your credit score has the potential to drastically alter your financial situation. A good credit score will help you get lower interest rates, better credit cards, and even help you rent an apartment. However, not everyone knows how a credit score is measured or many of the other significant aspects of a credit score. Credit scores were created to make it easier for lenders to make decisions. Credit unions and banks usually ask for clarification about how much of a risk of default you face on any loan you take out. This is why they look for signs in your borrowing past. For example, they'd like to know if you've borrowed money before and successfully repaid it. They'll even want to know if you've recently defaulted on a number of loans.

Lenders report your actions to credit bureaus when you apply for a loan, and the bureaus turn the information into credit reports. When it comes to credit scores, computer-generated algorithms can read all of this data and generate a score that lenders can use to determine the repayment probability. Rather than spending minutes poring through each individual credit report needed for a loan, lenders can quickly assess a person's creditworthiness by simply looking at their ratings.

Since they are young, some people have no borrowing history: they have never taken out a loan, used a credit card, or used any other form of credit. Lenders must take various credit ratings into account for these types of applicants. Leasing, energy bills, and other bills are examples of alternate payment history sources.

You should request those free credit reports to see what information they have on you. You'll still be able to see if there are any mistakes, which you can fix so that they don't impact your credit score.

Chapter 2. Differences about FICO and other

How Is FICO Score Calculated?

If you've ever looked up your credit score, you might have wondered why the numbers from each major credit bureau varied. Different lenders and borrowers can choose to report to different credit bureaus, in addition to the three major credit bureaus using different methods to calculate credit scores.

A credit card business will only report to Equifax, while a lender may report to both Trans Union and Experian. Another lender might not send any details to any of the credit bureaus. Creditors and lenders have the option of reporting to them, but they are not expected to do so. Payment history does not automatically go to the credit bureaus; instead, it goes to the creditors and lenders, and it is only reported to the bureaus if they want to do so. Certain items can be prioritized by different firms. An auto lender, for example, may place a greater emphasis on a person's payment history, while a mortgage company may place a greater emphasis on the person's job history. Other lenders may take a more balanced approach, examining a variety of factors and prioritizing them equally.

The criteria they have to choose from to calculate your credit score include:

FICO Score - Credit Score - As calculated

Payment history

35%

Amounts Due (level of indebtedness) 30%

Long credit history

15%

New credits (debts)

10%

Credit Mix 10%

1. Payment History – 35%

The most significant factor in determining your credit score is whether or not you have paid your bills on time.

Payment history accounts for 35% of your FICO ratings, according to FICO. Payment history provides details about your account expenses, such as the amount of accounts you've paid on time and any accounts that have gone past due. Work toward regularly making timely payments for revolving loans, such as credit cards, and instalment loans, such as student loans, to boost this portion of your credit score. It's also a good idea to devise a strategy for achieving a debt-free target.

These are warning signs to potential lenders that you may not be able to repay them.

2. Amounts Owed – 30%

The amount you owe is the second most significant factor in your credit score. It looks at how much of your usable credit you're using – also known as your "utilization ratio."

Less is better, but owing a small sum can be preferable to owing nothing at all because lenders want to assume that if you borrow money, you will be responsible and financially secure enough to repay it. Keep credit card balances low in relation to available credit and pay bills on time to increase this credit score factor. Lenders would view you as a high risk if you regularly max out your credit cards or approach your credit limits. It's also a good idea to figure out how much you'll have to pay off a credit card before adding to your debt.

3. Length of Credit History - 15%

15 percent of your FICO score is determined by the length of your credit history. This includes how long your accounts have been open and how long it has been since you last used them. Lenders will get a better understanding of a person's long-term financial behavior if they have a longer credit history.

Lenders can look at other variables such as bank accounts, job records, and residence history if you don't have a credit history. If you have a stable savings or checking account, for example, the bank would be more likely to lend you a credit card or loan. If you're still having trouble getting credit, consider getting a secured credit card, which uses the money you put in a secured deposit account as collateral, or an insured loan, which is a loan that allows you to put up an asset as collateral.

4. New Credit - 10%

Your credit score takes into account how many new accounts you've applied for lately, as well as how long it's been since you've opened a new account (opening a bunch at once will hurt your score),

Your FICO score is affected by the new loan by 10%. This refers to the amount of new credit requests you've made in the last 60-90 days, including recent big requests and new accounts you've opened.

Obtaining a large number of new credit accounts in a short period of time will harm your credit score. It will be seen as a sign of risk by lenders. Apply for new credit only when it makes financial sense for your situation and goals, rather than responding to any card offer with a low-interest promotional rate. If they refuse it the first time, take some time to focus on enhancing your credit score before reapplying.

5. Types of Credit in Use - 10%

The final factor in determining your credit score is whether you have a combination of various forms of credit (such as a car loan, mortgage, credit cards, store accounts and student loan). Lenders want to know that you can responsibly handle a variety of accounts.

The various forms of credit For 10% of your FICO score, you use an account. Having a diverse set of accounts, such as credit cards, home loans, and retail accounts, will indicate to lenders that you are a low-risk borrower. You can raise your credit score by opening different types of accounts, but only apply for credit when you really need it. Never apply for credit solely to improve your credit score.

Table of credit scores:

What Does a FICO Score Mean?

Outstanding

a thousand or more

740 to 790 Excellent/Excellent/Excellent/Excellent/Excellent/Excellent/

from 670 to 739

Bad 579 or less Regular 580 to 669

The Vantage Scoring Model

The Vantage Score model is the second most common scoring model today. Experian, Equifax, and Trans Union, the three credit bureaus, made a remarkable show of collaboration in 2006 when they agreed to create a rival to FICO in order to standardize credit scores. As a result, the number of credit ratings available to lenders and creditors has increased.

The Vantage Score model takes into account similar information as FICO, but weights it differently. To calculate your ranking, they consider one-time bill payments, keeping credit card balances low, and taking on too many new credit obligations. Vantage's biggest benefit for those who are new to credit is that they will create a score for you in as little as two months after you make your first credit card payment.

FICO ratings are not the same as standard credit scores. Using details from your personal credit reports, they use a proprietary system of algorithms to calculate your credit risk. Other businesses will sometimes pattern their credit scores to resemble a FICO credit score as closely as possible, but as FICO points out1, this can result in scores that differ by as much as 100 points from the industry norm.

Even a few points will influence whether or not you get a good interest rate and terms (saving you as much as thousands of dollars over the term of the loan or credit).

How Is Vantage Score Calculated?

Vantage Score and FICO use similar measures to assess the credit worthiness. The main differences are the weightings they assign to the various elements, as well as the fact that they use data from all three credit reporting bureaus to calculate your ranking. We'll take a look at their six scoring variables.

1. Payment History – Highest Weighting

With Vantage Score, your payment history is the best predictor of risk for you. This is given a 40% weighting in their model, making it twice as important as their most important category, or equal to the second and third categories combined.

At all costs, late payments must be avoided. These will last up to seven years on your credit report.

2. Age/Type of Credit – Extreme Weighting

This category combines the length of your credit history with the types of credit you have. Vantage Score considers you outstanding in this category if you can make on-time payments on a five-year auto loan while still servicing a 30-year mortgage and regular credit card bills.

It accounts for 21% of the algorithm, making it the second most important component.

3. Credit Utilization – Extreme Weighting

Simply divide your total balances by your available credit to arrive at this number. Maintain a level of less than 30% at all times. It's even cooler if you can get a ten percent discount.

4. Total Balances – Medium Weighting

Your total debt group is given 11 percent weighting by Vantage Score (whether it is current or delinquent). You'll get a better score in this category if you reduce your overall debt.

5. Low Weighting – Recent Behavior

This group receives 5% of the vote. It examines how many newly opened accounts you have as well as the number of hard inquiries you have received. When you have a higher number of hard inquiries, you are deemed to be a higher risk and you might be taking on significantly more debt.

6. Credit Available – Extremely Low Weighting

This group accounts for 3% of the total. The amount of credit you have available for use at any given time is referred to as available credit. The more credit you have, the more points you'll get in this group, which is the least significant.

Credit Karma is the most well-known company that uses Vantage Score's model these days. They provide a fully free service (which includes your credit report and credit score) to over a hundred million customers. They can even help you with credit monitoring.

Vantage Score is now available in updated versions as well. In the trended results, they changed their model in 2017. Today, if you are paying down your debt with higher installments, you will earn more points than someone who just pays the minimum monthly payment and is steadily growing credit card debt.

Chapter 3. How to Manage your Credit Cards

How to Find Credit Cards with Guaranteed Approval?

What does true mean by promised approval? All credit cards come with some form of basic requirements before you are issued by a business. A key factor in those so-called secured credit cards is that the qualification requirements are usually minimal.

Milestone Master Card – Less Than Perfect Credit Considered

The Milestone MasterCard provides a fast and easy application process and the use of all types of credit is encouraged. The Milestone Card may be used anywhere Visa is approved, according to the credit available.

Total Visa Card

The Full Visa Card is another card that does not need a security deposit and provides all the perks of a Visa full-service card. The card allows borrowers to have a current checking account, and a one-time service fee is charged.

The lines of credit available are based on your actual credit score and credit worthiness.

How to Use a Credit Card Responsibly?

Try not to use more than 30% of your credit card's limit

- Make sure to always make payments on time. Even if it is the minimum payment!

- If you have the means, do your best to try and pay off your credit card balance in full each statement (this is not really all that realistic, I certainly couldn't do this in the past. But if you can, do so!)

How to Find Right Credit Card for You?

Depending on your age and profession you will find certain credit cards more advantageous for your specific needs.

Credit cards to get a Balance transfer

Even as credit cards include the capacity accounts, stability switches. Credit card is one, which provides a low fee. If you happen to keep money, there is a stability switch a great way to go. The reduction in the promotional cost (and more the promotional span), the larger the appealing card is. You may require a credit rating that is genuine to qualify.

Subprime credit rating cards

Credit rating cards are among the credit rating card solutions. Those credit rating cards have been aimed, and such cards have expenses and hobby prices. As acceptance is short for people who have a credit rating that is awful, the terms are hard.

Student credit cards

Student Credit Rating cards are those specifically made that those teens have credit rating documents. Student credit rating cards may come, such as a cost or wages on balance transfers. College students commonly must be registered at a licensed 4-year university to become approved to get a student loan scorecard

Restricted cause cards

Utilize motive Credit cards that are restricted can handiest at locations. Rationale cards function using a fee and fund cost as credit rating cards. Gas credit rating cards and store credit rating cards are cases of motive credit scorecards that are restricted.

Secured credit rating cards

Secured credit cards are an alternative rating repute. Cards call for a protection deposit to be set on the card. It might be additional in some instances -- combined with a default, although the credit rating limitation on a credit rating card is equal to the amount of the deposit left on the card. It is worth noting that you predicted to create payments on your credit card balance.

How to Get an Instalment Loan While Still in Bankruptcy

If you just filed for bankruptcy last week, you will have a very tough time quickly re-establishing credit. If some time has passed, you have a good shot at getting started though. It may be that a little more waiting is required before you can qualify for new credit lines. Even a relatively small mistake like maxing out a credit card or missing a utility bill can harm your credit score. Some might try to repair their credit from transactions they didn't think would harm their credit like closing an old account or even applying for a new loan. Then there might some who are trying to repair their credit after a major transgression like the declaration of bankruptcy. According to the reasons that have harmed your credit score, the time taken for repair will differ. This isn't a precise estimate and is only used as examples for your understanding. The recovery period will depend on several factors, along with the existing information on your credit report. If you have a long-standing credit history of timely payments, it is easier to repair any damage. If your credit history is riddled with defaulting on payments, then it will take longer to fix any damage. Apart from this, your existing score matters too. Applicants that have either no credit or bad credit scores are seen to be high-risk borrowers, and that results in them having a decreased chance of being approved for a credit card or loan. Conversely, individuals with good credit scores are seen to be low-risk borrowers, and this increases the likelihood of them getting their applications approved. Credit scores by themselves do not control whether your loan request is approved or not. They are simply numbers created from a credit report. Lenders use them as a tool. Standards are set for what credit scores are acceptable, and the final decision is made. It does take a bit of time, but if you develop your credit well, that can make your credit scores improve and increase your chances of getting approval.

How to Get Lender to Remove A Lot Days Late?

If you are currently behind on payments, ask the creditor if you can negotiate for a lower settlement amount, which includes their removing the late payments from your credit record after you have settled your debt. If they still want the full amount, then you may need to catch up before you can do anything else. If you cannot pay back your late payments, ask the creditor if you can work out a new payment plan that includes removal of the late payment information after you finish making a set number of payments, such as the first twelve monthly payments for the next year.

If they still want the full amount first, then you will have to get up to date on the amount owed. Once you are up to date with your payments, you can contact the creditor and plead your case to remove the negative late payment information. If you have a long-term relationship with them, let them know.

How to Get Credit Card Offers?

A vast majority of lenders don't have offers that are clearly defined up front, instead they have a general loan package that can be tweaked based on the situation individuals who come to them find themselves in.

To maximize this strategy, you are going to want to make a list of the features you are absolutely going to need to be happy with a given loan and then call each lender you have already talked to and go down the list point by point. If you come across a lender who has an approach that appeals to you, let the other lenders know about it and see what they can do to either match or beat it. They know they are in a competitive business and if you are willing to force their hand, they will show you just how much they want your business.

Pre-approved offers: If you have not opted out of the system, and your credit isn't terrible, then putting in an application with one lender will likely trigger a barrage of competing offers from other lenders as creditors will happily provide your information to anyone and everyone who is interested in selling you on their services.

While this can be annoying in some cases, if you are looking for the best lender possible then it could be just what you need to pit several lenders against one another. Pre-screened offers can make it easier for you to compare relative costs or special offers as long as you do your due diligence with each and ensure that you aren't being hornswoggled by smoke and mirrors.

Ensure you have a loan estimate document: The loan estimate document was created by the Consumer Financial Protection Bureau to make it easier for borrowers to compare the various costs associated with individual loans and lenders. Its job is to standardize and simplify the way that lenders expose their fees so that you aren't comparing apples to oranges. The loan estimate document can be downloaded from ConsumerFinance.gov.

When and How to Open or Close A Credit Card

A major factor that plays into determining whether opening credit card accounts will be favourable to you or not is the credit utilization ratio. It is prudent to ensure that your credit utilization ratio is as low as possible. Essentially, you must make sure that you are using too much credit. You might be tempted to close certain credit card accounts, especially if you have managed to pay off all your credit card dues. However, don't do this. Don't allow the temptation to increase your spending get a hold of you. Your credit utilization ratio can increase when you close an account. So, if you don't trust yourself with a credit card, you can store it away for safekeeping or keep it out of your reach.

A Technique for Paying Off Your Credit Card Debt

If all your accounts have a similar interest rate, the Snowball Method might be a better option, but if you have one or two cards with a scandalously high interest rate, the Avalanche Method might be the right solution. It should be noted that both methods require that you have enough money to pay more than the minimum on your credit cards.

Avalanche method

Using this method, people use the extra money they get each month to pay off the debt at the highest interest rate, with all minimum payments remaining. By eliminating higher interest payments faster, you'll pay less interest over the next few months until the total debt is paid off. Once you have paid off your first high interest debt, find the next highest interest rate and repeat the process. Pay above the minimum amount as much as you can, so you can get out of debt faster.

Snowball method

By following this method, people instead of focusing on the highest debt, should first focus on paying off the card with the lowest debt until they reach the largest regardless of the interest rate. Then you work your way so you can pay the most you owe.

Paying debts with the lowest amounts first, you pay off those smaller payments quickly and have fewer bills to worry about. Finally, you should continue to pay the bills with the lowest balances until you have no debt left.

Chapter 4. Building the perfect credit profile

While this is going to be easier said than done in most situations, according to Experian, the ideal amount of credit utilization that you want is 30 per cent or less. While there are other ways to increase your credit utilization rating, paying off what you owe on time each month will also go towards showing you can pay your bills on time, essentially pulling double duty when it comes to improving your credit score. It will also make it easier to follow through on the following tips.

If you have a credit card that you use on a regular basis, say for example because it offers you reward points, so much so that you max it out each month, it may actually be hurting your credit even though you pay it off in full at the end of each month. This may be the case due to the way the credit card company reports to the credit bureau; depending on when they report each month it could show that your credit utilization rate is close to 100 per cent depending on what your credit line currently is, thus hurting your credit score. As such, paying off your credit card in two smaller chunks throughout the month can actually help boost your credit without costing you anything extra overall.

Increase your credit limit: If you aren't currently in a position to pay down your credit card balance, you can still improve your credit utilization rate by increasing your current credit limit. This is an easy way to improve your credit utilization rate without putting any more money out up front. If you do this, however, it is important that you don't take advantage of the increased credit line as if you find yourself up against the limit again you will be worse off than when you started. Open a new account: Improving your credit utilization rate is one of the best ways to start rebuilding your credit. If your current credit card company won't increase your credit limit you may way to try applying for another credit card instead. If your credit is not so hot then your rates are going to be higher, but this won't matter as long as you don't plan on using the card in the first place. Remember, credit utilization rate is a combination of your total available lines of credit so this can be a good way to drop your current utilization rate substantially, especially if you won't be able to pay off what you currently owe for a significant period of time. Spreading out these requests will give the inquiries time to drop off naturally and will prevent you from looking desperate to potential lenders which can also make it more difficult to get a new card.

Authorized users: If you don't have the credit to get a new credit card, or even to extend your current credit line, then your best choice may be to find someone you trust and ask them to become an authorized user on their card. While most people will likely balk at the idea, you may be able to pacify them by explaining that you don't need a copy of their card or have any intent on using it, simply being listed on the card is enough to improve your credit utilization rating.

What to do if your credit scores goes down

Plastic Money - The first thing you need to do to improve your score is to stop using plastic money. If you've already created a large invoice, you can order it, but no longer use the card. Reduce your purchases for a while until you are in control of the situation again.

Report - Request a report and rate the area you need to work on. You also need to carefully review the reports to determine if there are errors. Check for incorrect information. Has it corrected by writing to the office about it?

Pay your bills on time - use your salary to pay your bills on time. Don't be late in paying. Late payment not only involves fees and expenses but is also reflected negatively in the relationship.

Don't fall victim to scam repair - discover the federal law that governs this system. Some people fall victim to such repair agencies. It is better to face the situation alone. If necessary, contact the State Commission for more information on the procedure. You can also read books on credit. It's important to keep the situation under control before it gets worse and makes you fail.

Refinance Revolving Debt

Any time you pay off your credit cards your score is going to go up.

Refinancing your revolving debt with an instalment loan is a way to game the system into thinking you have less debt.

FICO doesn't give as much weight to instalment loans, so adding the equivalent instalment debt while paying off revolving debt will have an overall positive effect on your score.

Just don't go running up your cards while you're paying off your instalment loan or you'll end up with twice the debt.

That's a recipe for disaster.

Day 16 - Refinance Revolving Debt with a Home Equity Loan

Using a Home Equity Loan (HEL) to pay off your revolving debts will improve your credit scores for the same reason using any other instalment loan to pay off your revolving debt would work.

FICO gives less weight to instalment loan debt.

You just need to make sure you use a Home Equity LOAN and not a Home Equity Line of Credit (HELOC).

A HELOC is scored just like a credit card by FICO, so using it wouldn't improve your scores.

Just be sure to use it to pay down your debt and not as a way to get yourself into more debt.

If you're not disciplined enough to not run up your balances again, then this would not be a smart move for you.

I include it because it works, but you have to pick and choose what works for YOU.

Chapter 5. Personal or Business Credit Card?

A personal credit score will be between 300 and 850. A score in the high 700s will be an attractive customer for credit agencies. A high credit score can have many benefits. You can negotiate better deals, qualify for additional credit more easily, and be offered some of the best credit terms available. Business credit cards offer similar rewards to personal credit cards, but you will only get these if the business has a good credit score. Most of the rewards for business will be in the form of a cash back percentage on the purchases made with the business credit card. You are effectively saving money with every purchase. The business can often use the cash back to pay for reduced flight fares, which is highly beneficial if your employees need to travel for work.

Business credit card balances don't show on your personal credit unless you personally guarantee them or miss payments.

Therefore, any purchases made with a business credit card will not adversely affect your scores. Even if you max out your business credit card month after month, it will not hurt your personal credit score. Unfortunately, the balances you carry with your PERSONAL credit cards affects your scores more than almost anything else.

The Do's and Don'ts of Managing Your Credit

That is actually a very powerful statement: "Tell me what to do. It also means that people trust me to help them.

DO: Always, always pay on time. Considering that your payment history is the biggest percentage when it comes to calculating your credit score, it is crucial that you make all payments punctually. If possible, make credit card payments before the reporting date.

DON'T: Be late or miss a payment; once again, payment history is one of the biggest components used when calculating your FICO Score. Making late payments can lead to serious consequences. DO: Watch your usage of available credit. Remember that utilization plays a big role in your credit scoring.

DON'T: Max out any of your credit cards. If you have a few credit cards but one of them is your absolute favourite, try to spread out the usage. If one credit card is maxed out, don't be afraid to transfer balances so that you can meet the 30% mark. Also make sure that the credit card or cards with the higher limits get paid off first.

DO: Age your accounts. Simply, the older your accounts, the better. Recall that Length of History was a component of your credit scoring. Aging your accounts will help to improve your credit file and credit score.

DON'T: Close older accounts. It is far from a good idea to do this. Also try to avoid opening too many new accounts; this brings the age average down.

DO: Make sure to minimize new credit. You don't want to open up too many new accounts too fast. Doing so would affect the aging of your accounts as mentioned.

DON'T: Make too many inquiries. An inquiry is simply whenever you, or someone else, requests your credit file. A soft pull inquiry does not have the same potential for credit disaster as a hard pull possesses. A hard pull occurs when you request your credit file to apply for credit (credit cards, car, house etc.) A soft pull occurs when companies request your file in order to make you credit card offers and such.

DO: Mix up your accounts and add variety. If you were to submit a résumé to an employer, the more work experience and variety you presented, the more likely you are to be hired. By adding variety to your file, you are showing that you know how to manage your credit in more than one way.

The Secret to Success

The value of credit is highly underestimated and it is done so on purpose. If everyone knew the true value of credit and how to make it work for them, there would be an overflow of successful people and perhaps even more millionaires. The business of lending is one of the biggest industries on earth due to the trillions of dollars being exchanged at varying interest rates. Saving 1% on an interest rate can be the difference in tens of thousands of dollars. It is clear to see that credit is important and valuable. But let's discuss how it can make you successful.

Making powerful investments in life, such as real estate or opening up a business can take tons of money and it can take more money than most people have available. This is where the value of credit comes in. With a good credit score, making investments without having the cash is extremely possible. When you build your credit file exactly the way it's supposed to be, it makes it so much easier for lenders to decide to loan you money no matter what type of purchase or investment you wish to make.

When it comes to opening a business, banks are willing to give small business start-up loans to get a business off the ground, but it all depends on your credit score. They want someone who is guaranteed to repay the money, a Personal Guarantor. So no matter what you are doing: making a big purchase, starting up a new business, or being a real estate mogul, your credit will always be a major decision factor. This is the reason why credit is the secret to success and taking care of your credit can truly lead to the American Dream or at least financial stability. Many of the world's richest people were not born with money but made their fortune through knowledge and innovation.

Chapter 6. Fixing Your Credit Score Fast

Credit bureaus have 30 days to examine complaints and frequently concede to what lenders state about you, regardless of whether it's valid. Regardless of whether all parties concur that a mistake has been made, the errors can continue to manifest in your file on account of the automated idea of most credit reporting. You may need to contact creditors and the bureaus a few times to get mistakes erased. The process may take weeks; best case scenario, you may be taking on the conflict for quite a long time or even years. In case you're amidst attempting to get a mortgage, these errors can cause significant problems. You probably won't have sufficient opportunity to fix your report before the house drops out of escrow or you stall out with an interest rate a lot higher than you have the right to pay.

Issues, for example, these might entice you to turn to one of the numerous organizations that guarantee "moment credit fix" or that assurance to help your credit score. No authentic organization makes such guarantees or certifications, however, so any individual who employs one of these outfits is asking to be misled. There are, in any case, a developing number of certified administrations that can actually fix your credit report errors in 72 hours or less. Read on to learn more.

Fixing Your Credit in a Matter of Hours: Rapid Rescoring

Rapid rescoring administrations came about in light of the fact that such a large number of people were losing loans or paying an excess of interest on account of credit bureau mistakes. Before you get energized, however, you ought to learn what these administrations can and can't do:

- They can't manage you straightforwardly as a consumer—Rapid rescoring is typically offered by little credit-reporting agencies, which fill in as a kind of go between the bureaus and the lending experts. These agencies, which are frequently free, however, which may be auxiliaries of credit bureaus, provide uncommon administrations for loan officials and mortgage representatives, for example, blended or "3-in-1" credit reports. To profit by rapid rescoring, you should work with a loan official or mortgage representative who buys in to an agency that offers the administration.

- They can help you just in the event that you have proof, or if proof can be obtained—Rapid rescoring administrations aren't intended to help people who presently can't seem to begin the credit-fix process. You need something in writing, for example, a letter from the creditor recognizing that your account was reported as late when you were actually reality on time. (This is one reason that it's so necessary to get everything in writing when you're attempting to fix your credit.) If you don't have such proof, however, the creditor has recognized the error, some rapid recorders can get the proof for you. Nonetheless, that may add days or weeks to the process.
- They can assist you with getting errors fixed; however, they can't remove genuine negative things that are in dispute—also, you need proof that a mistake was made—not simply your say as much. If that the credit bureau is already researching your complaint regarding the error, the item typically cannot be included in a rapid rescoring process.
- They can't vow to support your score—"How Credit Scoring Works," sometimes removing negative

items can really hurt a score—strange as that may appear.

The scoring formula attempts to contrast you with people who have comparable credit histories. In the event that you've been lumped into the gathering with a bankruptcy or other dark spots on your report, you may find that your score falls when a portion of those negative items are removed. Rather than being at the highest point of the bankrupts' gathering, as such, you've dropped to the base of the following gathering—the people who have better credit. All the more commonly, removing an error probably won't help your score as much as you may have trusted and probably won't win you a superior interest rate. There are no assurances with rapid rescoring.

Quite a long time ago, brokers and other lending professionals could take care of these problems. In the days prior to the widespread utilization of a credit score, a broker or loan officer could mediate to persuade a lender to disregard mistakes or little imperfections on a client's credit file. Everybody included comprehended that credit report errors were common, and having an accomplished loan pro vouch for your creditworthiness could frequently complete an arrangement.

With the coming of credit scoring and automated loan processes, however, those chances to advocate for clients quickly evaporated. Lending professionals shared consumers' dissatisfaction when incorrect information continued to be reported by the bureaus—information that frequently hosed credit scores and brought about more awful rates and terms than the borrower merited. The mortgage brokers needed an approach to slice through the bureaucracy and accelerate the process. Free credit reporting agencies, with their littler, specific staffs, started to fill the need. Here's the means by which it works. Your broker loan or officer obtains evidence from you that a mistake has been done, and he sends that proof to the credit agency that provides the rapid rescoring service.

The recorders, thusly, have uncommon associations with the credit bureaus that enable their requests to be handled quickly. The rescoring service transfers proof of errors to unique departments at the credit bureaus, and the departments contact the creditors (typically electronically). In the event that the creditor concurs that an error was made, the bureaus quickly update your credit report. After that occurs, another credit score can be calculated. The expense for this service is typically somewhere close to $50 and $100 for each "trade line" or account that is remedied, albeit a few agencies provide the rescoring for no additional charge, as part of a part of services provided to lending professionals.

The presence of rapid rescoring does not change the way that you should be proactive about your credit. Months before applying for any loan, you have to order copies of your reports and start testing any errors. You likewise need to keep your correspondence about these errors. All things considered; rapid recorders typically require some kind of paper trail to pursue to prove to the bureau that the mistakes in fact exist. In any case, If that you wind up highly involved with getting a mortgage and an old problem repeats, rapid rescoring can assist you with disposing of the problem and spare the arrangement.

All in all, how would you discover one of these services? In case you're already managing a loan officer or mortgage broker, ask whether she approaches a rapid rescoring service. If that your lending pro has never known about rapid rescoring—it's an ongoing enough advancement that some haven't—request that her contact the agency that provides her organization with credit reports to check whether it's accessible.

Boosting Your Score in 30 to 60 Days

Rebuilding your credit can sometimes be an excruciatingly slow process, yet you can take a couple of easy routes that may increase your score in as meagre as a month or two, as talked about in the accompanying segments.

Pay Off Your Lines of Credit & Credit Cards.

Probably the fastest approaches to support a score is to lower your debt use proportion—the distinction between the amounts of revolving credit that is accessible to you and the amount that you're utilizing. One straightforward approach to improve your proportion is to redistribute your debt. In the event that you have a big balance on one card, for instance, you could transfer probably a portion of the debt to different cards. It's usually better for your scores to have little balances on a number of cards than a big balance on a solitary card. You additionally could explore getting a personal instalment loan with your nearby credit association or bank, and utilize the cash to pay down your cards. Applying for the loan may affect your scores a piece; however, that is probably going to be more than offset by the development to your scores from lessening the balances on your credit cards. (Credit scoring formulas are substantially more delicate to the balances on revolving debt, for example, credit cards, than to the balances on instalment loans.)

Utilize Your Credit Cards Lightly

A big difference between your balances and your limits is what the scoring formula likes to see —and it doesn't really care whether you pay off your balances in full each month or carry them from month to month. What makes a difference is the amount of your credit limits you're really utilizing at some random time. A few people demand they've supported their scores by paying off their cards in full a couple of days before their announcement closes. In the event that their credit card backers, as a rule, send out bills around the 25th, for instance, these people check their balances online about seven days prior and pay off whatever's owed, in addition to a couple of bucks to cover any charges that may manifest before the 25th. When the bills are really printed, their balances are pretty close to zero. (In the event that you utilize this method, simply make sure you make a second payment after your announcement shows up if your balance isn't already zero. That will make sure you don't get damaged with late charges—and truly, that can occur, despite the fact that you made a payment before in the month.)

Concentrate on Correcting the Big Mistakes on Your Credit Reports

If that another person's bankruptcy, collections, or charge-offs are showing up on your report, you will probably profit by having those removed. If that an account you closed is reported as open, then again, you'll probably need to disregard it. Having an account filed as "closed" on your file can't support your score and may hurt it.

Utilize the Bureaus' Online Dispute Process

Some credit-fix veterans swear they get faster results along these lines, however regardless, you'll have to make printouts of all that you send to the bureaus and each correspondence you get from them.

Check whether You Can Have Your Creditors Update Positive Accounts or to Report

Not all creditors report to every one of the three bureaus, and some don't report reliably. If that you can get a creditor to report an account that is in good standing; however, you may see a quick knock in your score.

Chapter 7. Mind-set of money Management

The Importance of Money Management

Do you find yourself with different credit cards, a mortgage, and an auto loan?

There are methods to help you make this manageable. It takes time to discover the ins and outs of it and twist your budget so that it can satisfy your needs:

You Know Where Your Money Is Going

If you handle your money well, you will manage to make early payments, and avoid surpassing the limit on the credit card.

When you stick to your budget, these methods will assist you to save money.

This prevents you from spending much money.

A Better Plan of Retirement

When you save now and manage your money in the right way, it will benefit you in the long term. First, it will force you to look into the future and look into your retirement plans.

When you implement your money management skills, you will be building yourself a strong retirement plan. The money that you save and invest will grow as time goes by.

Allows You to Concentrate On Your Goals

You will avoid unnecessary expenditure that doesn't support achieving financial goals. If you are dealing with limited resources, budgeting makes it complex to fulfil your ends.

You Organize Your Spending and Savings

When you divide your income into different types of expenditure and savings, a budget will allow you to remain aware of the type of expenditure that drains the portion of your money. This way, it is simple for you to set adjustments. Good money management acts as a reference for organizing receipts, bills, and financial statements. Once you organize all your financial transactions, you will save effort and time.

You Can Speak To Your Partner about Money

If you do share your income with your spouse, then a budget can be the best tool to show how money is spent.

This increases teamwork to work on a common financial target and prevents arguments on the way money is used. Creating a budget together with your spouse will help you to avoid conflict and eliminate personal conflicts on the way money is spent.

It Determines Whether You Can Take On Debt and How Much

Taking on debt isn't a bad thing, but it is important, especially if you cannot afford it. A budget will indicate the amount of debt load you can take on without getting stressed.

Budgeting

When you budget, you get the chance to single out and eliminate unnecessary spending such as on penalties, late fees, and interests. These little savings can increase with time.

A budget refers to a plan that takes into account your monthly cash flow and outflow. This is a snapshot of what you own, and what you expect to spend, and which will allow you to realize your financial goals by assisting you in highlighting you're saving and spending.

Creating a budget is the most crucial aspect of financial planning. The amount of money you have doesn't indicate how much money you make, but instead, it is how effective your budgeting is. If you want to take care of your finances, then you will have to understand where your money is flowing to. Contrary to popular belief that budgeting is hard, it isn't, and it doesn't eliminate the fun from your life. A budget will save you from an unexpected financial crisis and a life of debt.

Monitor Your Expenses and Income

The first thing to building a budget is to determine the amount of money you have and what you are spending it on. By monitoring your expenses, you will manage to classify how you spend your money. Planning how you spend your money is critical because you can tell how much you want to spend in every category. You can monitor your income and expenses by creating a journal, spreadsheet, or cash book. Every time you make money, you can monitor it as income, and every time you spend money, you can track it as an expense.

If you use a debit card, try to track back three months of your spending to get a comprehensive picture of your expenditure.

Evaluate Your Income

The next stage is to assess your income. You can do this by computing the amount of income you get via gifts, scholarships, etc.

Determine Your Expenses

Once you know your monthly income, next is to determine the total of your expenses. First, you need to define what your fixed, variable expenses are. Fixed expenses, sales, and bills have the same price every month. The fixed expenses comprise of car payments, internet, and rent. Variable expenses refer to costs that change, such as utilities and groceries.

Be sure to include payments of debt in your budget. Find out the amount that you can contribute towards your debts to make sure that you are on the correct path to financial stability. Handling debts and savings go hand in hand.

Building a Saving Strategy

It is quite easy to forget to save money. Keep in mind that you always pay yourself first. Give it a try using 10-20% of your income savings. Since savings increase, you can choose to include money that you didn't spend in the budget to save.

Many people know how to manage the little money they get when the month ends, but they find it hard to save when they have a tight budget. If you look at finance articles online, you will see different types of saving methods—right from freezing all spending to packing your own lunch for a month. But how can you determine which one's work? In this part, you will learn easy money-saving strategies you can implement and how you can make them work for you:

Stay Out Of Debt

Being debt free will help you to save cash; if you can pay off all your debt, you will get the chance to organize your debt.

The stats on eliminating debt can be shocking. For example, the Claris poll showed that only 22% of people attempted this strategy, and 26% reported that it worked for them. In other words, this strategy can help you save money.

Staying out of debt can save you a good sum of cash, but many people find it hard to pay off their debts.

Be a Minimalist

Adopting a minimalist approach is a type of voluntary simplicity. It requires a person to cut down on costs so that they concentrate on what is important. A minimalist's life generally means owning a smaller house, fewer "toys", and fewer clothes. But it also implies minimal work and more time to do the things that you like.

This is a great saving strategy that works even for those who don't want to use it. A minimalist approach can be the effect of other methods to save. In most cases, many people scaled their life to stick to their budget. Then, with time, they discovered that their simple lifestyle helped them save more.

There are various misconceptions about minimalism. A blog about minimalism jokes that minimalists live in small apartments and don't have jobs, cars, TVs, or more than 100 objects.

The purpose of minimalism is to free yourself from issues in life that aren't important. It is not focused on sacrifice; it merely involves eliminating things that you don't want to have in life or creating room for things that you care about. As a result, living with fewer items can make you feel satisfied.

If you aren't sure whether you can deal with this kind of life, you can start small and slowly identify a few things in your life that you don't want. For example, if your wardrobe is filled with many things, perhaps throw out or donate some clothes. Whatever you decide to do, make sure that you don't simplify your life by surrendering on the things you value or treasure; instead, choose things that require the most work for the least reward.

Since they have worked for other people, there is a big chance that they will work for you too. However, make sure that you don't jump in and try all the methods at once—just select strategies that you believe may work for you.

Investing your Money

Investing your money gives you a chance to grow your money, and even make more than what you have. However, not everyone who decides to invest their money makes profits; some have lost tons of money in the process. There is a different way to invest your money, and this will introduce you to some of the most common strategies for investment:

Online investing can be a quick and convenient method that is more affordable than other methods. But before you can handle your online investment, you need to ask yourself several questions:

Online investing is designed for everyone. By choosing this option, you hold the responsibility to research all investments and make all investment decisions regarding your online account. If you don't feel okay as that kind of investor, you could be comfortable working with a financial advisor. If you like to manage your investment portfolio and feel secure that you have enough knowledge, you may decide to go with online investment.

Stop Spending

If you can't stop spending money that you don't have, this book will only temporarily fix your problems, if it is even able to do that. If you have a habit of living out of your means and buying things you cannot afford, this is your chance to fix that. If you want to fix your credit and improve your life financially, you must take care of these things. So sit tight, make a budget, and find something that works, and cut up those maxed out credit cards if you have to.

Chapter 8. All about Your Credit Score

Your credit report is actually more complicated than it may appear at first glance, simply because you are actually dealing with reports from three different agencies, Tran's union, Experian and Equifax.

Anatomy of a credit report

While the three major credit reports are going to vary somewhat, information is always going to be grouped into four major categories, these are credit inquires, creditor information, public record information and personal information.

Personal information: The is going to include things like you name and any aliases you use, your social security number, date of birth, employment information and your current and previous addresses.

Public record information: This will include any currently pending legal issues related to your current financial situation. This can include bankruptcies, wage garnishments, judgments and liens. A Tran's union report will also show the approximate date when these details will be removed from your report.

Creditor information: This will show all of your debts that have been turned over to a collection agency and all of the lines of credit that you currently have. Additionally, you will find details outlining the status of the account in question, if you share responsibility on any of the accounts, your current balance, payment history, credit limit and if the account is currently past due. Typically, positive and negative accounts will be grouped together.

If you have accounts that are negatively affecting your credit, it is important to keep in mind that you can dispute any of these issues with the credit reporting company. Barring that they will fall off your report after the issue has been resolved for seven years.

Each of your accounts can be classified in the following ways: if any of your accounts are listed as charged off, that means that the account has been written off from the creditor as a loss. While this means you may not have to pay off the account. A revolving account is the classification given to credit cards, you don't need to pay these in full each month and can instead revolve them and just pay the interest.

An instalment account is the classification given to loans or other accounts that involved fixed payments. An open account is the classification given to accounts that force you to pay the total balance off each month. A collection account is the classification given to any account that has been transferred to a debt collection agency, this will even show on accounts that you have settled the debt for in the past seven years.

Credit inquiries: This part of your credit report includes a list of every agency that has reviewed your credit report in the past seven years. There are two different types of inquiries, hard inquiries and Soft inquiries.

Credit report codes: The following is a list of codes you may see on your credit report and what they mean.

- CURR ACCT: This means the account is in good standing and current.

- CUR WAS 30-2: This means the account is currently in good standing but has been late by 30 days or more at least twice.
- PAID: This means the account is currently inactive and has been paid off
- CHARGOFF: This means the account has been charged off.
- COLLECT: This means the account has been sent to collections.
- BKLIQREQ: This means the debt has been forgiven due to bankruptcy.
- DELINQ 60: This means the account is at least 60 days past due.

The Fair Credit Acts

FCRA: The FCRA does more than just provide you with a free credit report each year, it also regulates the various credit reporting organizations and helps to ensure that the information they gather on you is both accurate and fair. This means that if you see inaccurate information on your credit report, and report it to the relevant agency, they are legally required to look into the matter and resolve it, typically within 30 days. The same applies to agencies or organizations that generally add details to your credit report.

While this won't help you with that particular lender, if the information is inaccurate you will at least know where to go to clear up the issue. Additionally, if you report an inaccuracy and the credit reporting agency ignores your request you can sue them to recover the damages or a minimum of $2,500. You may also be able to win an additional amount based on punitive damages and legal fees and any other associated costs. You must file legal proceedings within 5 years of when this occurs.

Fair Credit Billing Act: This federal law is part of what is known as the Truth in Lending Act. Its purpose is to provide safeguards to consumers when it comes to unfair billing and make it clear how any errors must be corrected. This law is useful if you are charged for things you didn't purchase, are charged an inaccurate amount for products or services, you didn't receive and item you paid for, payments made aren't reflected in amounts owed or if your statements are sent to an inaccurate address.

To take advantage of this law, the first thing you need to do is to send a physical letter to the billing inquiries address that the creditor provides. You need to ensure the creditor receives your letter within 60 days from the date the error shows up on your statement. Some creditors allow for disputes to be handled online but utilizing this option can nullify your rights through this law so it is not recommended. The creditor will then have 30 days to acknowledge they received your letter to either correct the mistake or tell you why they think it is valid. If they turn down your request you are then allowed to ask for all the documentation saying why they turned you down.

A subset of this law is what is known as the Hidden Gem Law, this means you can dispute any transaction made within 100 miles of your home, or anywhere in your home state, which exceeds $50. As long as you make a good faith effort to dispute the transaction, and return the item or stop using the service, then the company will likely refund the transaction.

Fair Debt Collection Practices Act: This is another law that benefits consumers when it comes to debt collector actions. This includes not only debt collection agencies but also their attorneys. This law prevents debt collection agencies from contacting you if you have requested that the debt be validated, contacting you instead of your attorney (if applicable) calling before 8 am or after 9 pm, contacting you at work, calling constantly, reporting false information to credit bureaus, embarrassing you in an effort to collect the debt, adding your name to a list of debtors, threatening legal action they can't actually follow through on, misrepresentation or contacting you after you have sent a letter requesting that they stop or saying that you will not pay the debt in question.

If the debt collector breaks these rules or acts in other ways they are not allowed then you can file a private lawsuit and be recouped costs, fees and damages. What's more, you don't even need to prove damages and you will likely be awarded a minimum of $1,000.

Chapter 9. Harming My Credit Score

It is also necessary to take a closer look at some of the different parts that are going to end up harming the credit scores that we have. If you are in the process of fixing your credit, you want to make sure that you are careful and that you are not going to end up doing something that will harm your credit in the process. Some of the different things that we are able to watch out for when it comes to harming your credit score include:

Paying Late or Not at All

One of the worst things that you can do when it comes to your credit score is paying late on anything. About 35 percent of your score is going to be about your history of making payments or not on time. Consistently being late on these payments is going to cause a lot of damage to your credit score.

What is even worse than paying late is not paying at all? If you decide to completely ignore your cards and other bills and not pay them at all, then you are going to be in even more trouble as well. Each month that you miss out on a payment for your credit card, you are going to end up with one month closer to helping your account be charged off.

If you ever want a chance to get your credit score up at all, especially if you are hoping to get it up to 800 or higher, then you have to stop the late payments. This is going to be a bad thing because it shows that you are not willing to pay your money back, and they are less likely to give you some more money in the process.

For those who are struggling with making payments, whether these payments are often late or they don't come in at all, it is time to get a budget in place. You are living above your means, and this is never a good sign to getting your score up to where you would like. When you are able to get your budget in place and can start paying your debts on time, you will be able to get that credit score higher in no time.

Having an Account Charged Off or Sent to Collections

Next on the list is having your accounts charged off. When creditors are worried that you will never pay in your bills for loans or credit cards, they are going to use a process known as charging off your accounts. A charge off means that the insurer has pretty much given up on ever hearing from you again. This is actually one of the absolute worst things out there when it comes to your credit score.

Another issue is when one of your accounts is sent off to collections. Creditors are often going to work with debt collectors in order to work on collecting a payment out of you. Collectors could send your account to collections after, but sometimes before, charging it all off. This is never a good thing, no matter if the account is charged off at that time, either.

If you are to the point of your bills going to collections or being charged off, this means that you have not just missed one or two payments. It means that you have gone so long without paying the whole thing that the company figures they are never going to get it back. They have probably either written it off as a tax break, or they have sold it to a credit collection company that will be bothering you a lot in the future.

Filing Bankruptcy

This is a bit extreme that you should try to avoid at all costs. Bankruptcy is an extreme measure, and it is going to cause a lot of devastation to the score that you are working with. It is also going to be on your record for seven to ten years. It is a good idea to seek some alternatives, like working with counselling for consumer credit, before filing bankruptcy.

It is best if you are able to do everything that you can to avoid bankruptcy at all costs. It may seem like the best idea to work with. You assume that when you declare bankruptcy, you can just walk away from all of the debt that you have, and not have to worry about it ever again. This is not really how this whole process is going to work for you at all, though.

To avoid bankruptcy, you need to go through and learn how to work with a budget and figure out the best ways to manage your money, no matter what the income is that you are working with. The bankruptcy seems like an easy way to get out of the debt, but it haunts you for many years afterward, can make getting credit later on almost impossible, and it will really not solve the underlying problem that got you to this situation.

High Balances or Maxed Out Cards

We always need to take a look at the balances that we are going to have on our credit cards all of the time. The second most important part that comes with our credit score is the amount of debt that is on them, and that is going to be measured out by credit utilization. Having high balances for credit cards, relative to the credit limit that you are working with, will increase the utilization of credit and will make your credit score goes down. For example, if you have a limit of $10,000 on a card, but the balance is at $9500 or higher, then your score is not going to reflect in a positive manner with this one.

We also need to make sure that we are not maxing out or going over the limit when it comes to our credit cards. Credit cards that are over the limit or that have been maxed out are going to make the credit utilization that you have at 100 percent. Make sure to pay down those debts as fast as you can to maintain your credit score and keep it from going over the top.

Closing Credit Cards

There are a few ways that closing your card is going to end up with a decrease in your credit score. When you close that card, the credit limit you get to work with is going to end up at $0, while your balance is still going to be the same. This is going to make it look like you have been able to max out the credit card, which is going to cause your score to drop a bit. If you want to close your account, then you need to make sure that you pay off the balance before you close it.

What will happen when you close out your credit cards that are old is another thing to study. Closing up old cards, especially some of the oldest cards, are going to make your history seem like it is a lot shorter than it is. And finally, we need to be careful about closing cards that have available credit. If you have more than one credit card to work with, some that have balanced and some without these, then closing the cards that do not have a balance is going to increase the credit utilization. You can just keep those all out of the way, and see your credit report go up.

Not Having Enough Mix on the Report

While this is not as big of a deal as some of the other options, you will find that having a good mix of credit is going to be about 10 percent of your credit score at the time. If you have a report that only has one or two things on it, such as either credit cards or loans, then it is likely the score you are working with will be affected in some way or another.

The more that you are able to mix up your accounts and get them to have a lot of different things on them, the better. You don't want to overextend yourself, but having a mix of loans, mortgage, credit cards, and more, that you pay off each month without fail, is going to be one of the best ways that you can raise your credit score without causing harm or paying too much in the process.

This is something that often happens; naturally, the longer you work on your credit score. You may have a few credit cards. And then you take out a loan for a car and pay it off. Maybe you need a loan for a vacation or for some home improvement so you will have those accounts. And then get a mortgage too.

Applying for Too Much

Another thing that is going to count on your report is the credit inquiries. These will take up about 10 percent of the score that you work with. Always keep the applications for credit to a minimum, so this doesn't end up harming you along the way.

In some circumstances, this is not going to harm you too much. For example, if you have a good credit score and you want to apply for a mortgage, you will want to apply for a few mortgages and shop around a bit. If you do these close together, then it is not going to be seen as bad because the lender will assume this is what you are doing, rather than you taking on too much or that you have been turned down. You can also explain this to them easily if they ask.

Chapter 10. Increase Credit Limit

One of the least utilized strategies for lowering your debt utilization is a credit limit increase.

All you need to do is call your lender and ask if a credit limit increase is available for your account. Most people don't know that a customer service representative will pull up your entire account before they even answer the phone. They use caller ID to identify you, then have you prove your identity. Once proven, they have all your past conversations, your limits, balances, and possible upgrades available.

They just won't tell you unless you ask. By requesting a credit limit increase you're effectively increasing your available credit without increasing your balance.

For example, if you have one card with a $500 limit and $250 balance, then you're at 50% utilization.

If you get a $500 limit increase, then you have $1000 limit with a $250 balance. That brings your utilization down to only 25% instantly!

The lower your utilization, the higher your scores. With a secured card you simply increase your deposit.

For a regular credit card, make sure you make timely payments for at least 6 months, though 9 months is better. Make sure you keep your card under 50% utilization on all your cards. They won't approve you if you're maxed out or have missed payments within the past year. If they ask you what you're going to use the money for, don't say gambling, or anything irresponsible.

Say you're trying to improve your FICO scores or that you just got a raise and wanted to buy some new furniture. If they ask how large an increase you would like, ask them how much you qualify for. They can tell you after a minute or so.

If you're approved, then you just raised your credit scores with a phone call.

Become an Authorized User

A very simple yet effective technique for boosting your credit scores it to "piggyback" on someone else's credit history and become an Authorized User (AU) on their account.

An AU account is not like a Joint Account.

With a Joint Account both you and the primary holder can add to the credit balance, but you're also both liable for the debts.

If, for example, the primary files for bankruptcy protection, then you will be on the hook for the full balance.

You should avoid Joint accounts at all costs.

With an Authorized User account, only the primary card holder is liable for the debt.

However, the trade line appears on BOTH credit reports.

This is a great way to start your children's credit education, too.

The overnight addition to a credit's age, limit, and payment history can boost a score hundreds of points.

AU accounts are so effective for boosting credit scores that many unscrupulous credit services actually sell them as "Seasoned Trade lines".

First of all, buying a trade line for the purpose of qualifying for financing, like a home mortgage, is fraud. You could go to jail or receive a hefty fine.

Second, FICO knows about Seasoned Trade lines and has made adjustments. When those adjustments hit the scoring model lenders use, then those trade lines will become worthless.

Third, you don't need to buy trade lines anyway. Simply ask a family member, or someone you've shared an address with, to add you as an AU.

Tell them you don't need or want a card, but you want your credit score to benefit from their good credit history.

Look for a card from a major lender with a high limit, low balance, and perfect payment history. The older the card the better.

Refinance Revolving Debt

Any time you pay off your credit cards your score is going to go up.

Refinancing your revolving debt with an instalment loan is a way to game the system into thinking you have less debt.

FICO doesn't give as much weight to instalment loans, so adding the equivalent instalment debt while paying off revolving debt will have an overall positive effect on your score.

Just don't go running up your cards while you're paying off your instalment loan or you'll end up with twice the debt.

That's a recipe for disaster.

Day 16 - Refinance Revolving Debt with a Home Equity Loan

Using a Home Equity Loan (HEL) to pay off your revolving debts will improve your credit scores for the same reason using any other instalment loan to pay off your revolving debt would work.

FICO gives less weight to instalment loan debt.

You just need to make sure you use a Home Equity LOAN and not a Home Equity Line of Credit (HELOC).

A HELOC is scored just like a credit card by FICO, so using it wouldn't improve your scores.

Just be sure to use it to pay down your debt and not as a way to get yourself into more debt.

If you're not disciplined enough to not run up your balances again, then this would not be a smart move for you.

I include it because it works, but you have to pick and choose what works for YOU.

Credit Builder Loans

Some lenders offer a secured loan program designed to help you rebuild your credit.

They're called Credit Builder Loans.

This is a very effective, all be it slow, method for boosting your scores. It's slower because it's an instalment loan. Installment loans have less of an impact on your credit score.

Be that as it may, over 6-12 months you will see a credit score increase. That's because you need a few instalment loans to improve the "Credit Mix" which is responsible for 10% of your credit score.

Here's how your scores are determined:

FICO SCORES IMAGE

Ideal ratio is:

2-4 credit cards

A car loan, home loan, and personal loan

1-2 retail cards

The credit builder loan completes the personal loan portion of the equation.

Here's how it work;

The amount you borrow is deposited into an escrow account. You can't touch it until the loan is paid. You make your regular payments each month, building your credit score as you go. When you're done paying, you get the full balance plus interest, to do with as you please.

Traditional features include:

Loan amounts from $500-$3000

12-24 month terms

Loan funds earn dividends

Loan interest rate is fixed at 5%

So, for example, a $1000 loan at 5% over 18 months would equal payments of $57.79.

The terms may change from bank to bank so you need to shop around.

Credit Scoring Models

These are specialized agencies that develop scoring formats for credit bureaus. According to the Federal Statistics, there are over 50 of them in the United States. Of that, only FICO, a model designed by Fair Isaac Company, is widely used and accepted everywhere. It is often adopted by the three most popular credit bureaus in the country too. Fairly, FICO is trailed by Vantage, Community Empower, Trans union, Xpert, Insurance, and some others.

Due to this diversity, it is impossible to generate an all-purpose method of calculating credit scores. So, it would be impossible to tell how each company measures your credit performance concisely. It is clear however, these scoring models usually generate 3-digit as your credit score, which means you may rank anywhere between 300- 850 (or 950).

Chapter 11. The Importance of a Good Credit Score

A good relationship is significant for enhancing the creditworthiness of the market. It can help you in many ways and talk about your clean background. It reflects your personality and your character. Employers also prefer someone with a good score and a clean relationship. It is synonymous with sensitivity and responsibility. If you're at a loss and don't know how to improve your score, check out our credit guide.

How to Get Help?

At this point, as you read this article, you may experience the following problems.

- A poor or falling credit rating.
- Think about foreclosure or filing for bankruptcy.
- Invoices or credit card loans over the limit or pending.
- Threats for non-payment of bills, loans or mortgages.

Faced with one of these problems, you can get help from a variety of sources. These financial difficulties are common and can force you to lose your way. Several companies and agents are waiting to attract such gullible customers. They can mislead you and cause you further difficulties. You could work in your interest instead of in your interest. Several agencies of this type have unsatisfied customers who have been deceived. If you want to resolve your situation and work on the current financial situation, you need to read the relevant guide. Here are some ways you can improve your scores.

Tips to Improve Your Score

Plastic Money - The first thing you need to do to improve your score is to stop using plastic money. If you've already created a large invoice, you can order it, but no longer use the card. Reduce your purchases for a while until you are in control of the situation again.

Report - Request a report and rate the area you need to work on. You also need to carefully review the reports to determine if there are errors. Check for incorrect information. Has it corrected by writing to the office about it?

Pay your bills on time - use your salary to pay your bills on time. Don't be late in paying. Late payment not only involves fees and expenses but is also reflected negatively in the relationship.

Don't fall victim to scam repair - discover the federal law that governs this system. Some people fall victim to such repair agencies. It is better to face the situation alone. If necessary, contact the State Commission for more information on the procedure. You can also read books on credit. It's important to keep the situation under control before it gets worse and makes you fail.

Importance of a Good Credit Score?

The credit score is a numerical expression for the statistical analysis of credit files. In simple terms, this number will help you prove your creditworthiness. The score measures past ability to repay loans and manage previously granted loans. It is usually based on the reporting information of the credit bureau. You will rely on wounds to reduce losses when it comes to bad debt. It is the outcomes that can determine who is eligible for a loan and which interest rates are most appropriate, including the credit limits that individuals receive.

Credit scores can also say a lot about your character and personality and linger forever. You will never benefit from poor results in financial situations that must occur throughout your life. You can also use numbers to evaluate employers, which makes having a good score very important. It will represent your level of responsibility and sensitivity.

When buying a home: a home is a huge investment that can be very difficult to make. A home loan may be needed to make your dreams come true.

When buying a car: vehicle loans are among the most popular. Auto loans don't seem to be home loans. It is, therefore, possible to get along with bad credit scores. However, if you have bad credit, you will end up paying very high yield loans with your auto loan. The deposit is also higher for you if you have a band score.

When starting a business: Just like buying a house or car, financial support may be needed to start a business. The credit rating depends on your eligibility for that loan. This can seriously affect your ability to access a corporate loan when it is needed.

Looking for work: Nowadays, employers also run credit checks when they want to hire new employees. It is especially common in the financial sector and government institutions. A negative score can be an obstacle to this job, so it is important to maintain good credit scores.

You will also find it very important to check your credit report. A thorough review helps to identify errors. You will likewise get numerous tips and guidance on the best way to improve your credit ratings to keep up a cleaner register before you need money or business help. There are excellent websites out there that will help you check and calculate your scores and even get a free copy of them.

Before doing any real estate business, you need to know a few things about your balance. First, a copy of all three credit reports (Trans Union, Equifax and Experian) is required, which can be easily found online in this era of computer information.

The primary concern you need to search for in your momentum reports is the point at which you have recorded antagonistic data. "Unwanted information" includes things like late payments, collections, judgments, etc. If you have negative information about your relationships and have the money to pay for them, do it immediately. The better your credit, the more business you can do. However, as mentioned above, you can do business if you have bad credit. It's easier if you don't.

The accompanying table will enable you to comprehend where your credit is found:

Credit score / rating

700 or more / excellent (A + credit)

This score indicates that in the past three years, there have been no significant delays (60 days or more) for any type of loan payment. These people can get slightly better interest rates on some types of loans.

699-660 / Very good (credit)

659-620 / Voucher (one credit)

These values do not result in significant payments (60 days or more) overdue for a mortgage loan in the past two years and only a few small delays in loan payments over the past two years. These people can quickly get "market interest rates" on all types of loans, including public loans. Bankruptcies must be resolved and resolved for four years to be classified as "good".

619-590 / Fair (credit B)

This score indicates some significant delays (60 or more days) for a mortgage loan in the past two years and widespread minor delays in loan payments over the past three years. These people receive slightly higher interest rates for all types of loans, except for public loans (FHA, VA), which are not based solely on credit scores.

589-480 / Bad (credit C)

This score indicates MANY significant delays (60 days or more) overdue for a mortgage in the past two years and widespread MAJOR payments (60-90 days) for loan payments over the past three years. People with a C loan generally receive higher interest rates and higher equity or a higher down payment for all types of loans except public loans.

In most cases, 520 is the type of approval limit for portfolio loan buyers whose loans are led by actions.

Bankruptcies must be paid at the time of applying for a loan to be classified as "bad". Current amortizations, bad debts and sentences sometimes don't have to be repaid to get a mortgage. However, the penalty is a small pool of lenders, high-interest rates and stiff prepayment penalties if you refinance within three years.

Another factor in deciding your financial assessment is the number of solicitations you have. Numerous applications are dismissed because the candidate has an excessive amount of solicitations. As a general rule, "too many" requests are defined as more than 6-8 requests in your credit report. Credit bureaus have informed creditors that a person with more than this in their credit report is jumping around looking for credit, generally indicating that they are desperate or inattentive. Of course, they never think that you could simply look for the best loan.

If you have more than 6-8 requests in your credit reports, the new FCRA (Fair Credit Reporting Act) states that no requests can remain in your report for more than a year. If your report shows previous requests, you can remove duplicate requests.

It is essential to know your balance. If your score is between 620 and 700 or more, you can negotiate better conditions and interest rates on your loans. But if your credit is lower, you can still get credit, but all you have to do is "turn" and take a higher interest rate until your credit improves.

Before doing business, we cannot stress the importance of knowing your balance.

1. A borrower with a score of 680+ is considered for an A + loan. This type of loan includes the essential subscription, probably through a "computerized automated subscription" system, which is completed in a few minutes and can be completed in a few days.
2. A borrower with a score below 680 but over 620 will find that lenders take a closer look when applying for a loan. Additional credit documents and explanations may be requested before making a subscription decision.
3. A borrower with a score below 620 can be excluded from the best loan rates and conditions. These borrowers are usually redirected to alternative funding sources.

Remember, just because your credit isn't A +, with patience and some creative funding, you can still do the business you want to do. Your credit can and will consistently change, and as you begin working together and reimbursing these loan specialists, it will bit by bit increment. This makes financing your offers simpler and more straightforward. Be quiet and constant and recall the significance of knowing your equalization.

Chapter 12. How to Boost Your Credit Score

You need to know what is in your credit report before you can find out what you need to do to change it.

Check the credit report

The credit score provides a snapshot of your credit status and is determined by a series of factors that can be divided into the following categories: credit history - How long have you been using credit?

Payment History

Do you have a history of paying on time?

Credit amount - How much do you do and how much do you owe?

Check over your credit report with a fine-tooth comb: verify that the amount due for each account is accurate. And look for all the accounts you paid off that still show as outstanding issues. Pay particular attention to any requests for recent information that you have not authorized. Before an endorsing creditor, or someone pretending to be you, for an account, they will make a request that will be indicated on your credit report.

Checking your credit report on a regular basis, at least once a year, is a good way to collect any cases where you could be the target of identity theft - or the credit bureau has accidentally mixed your story with someone similar name.

Pay early and often (or at least, on time)

Credit reports record payment habits on all types of bills and extended credit, not just credit cards. And sometimes these objects show up on their own official report, but not that of another. Old, unpaid gymnastic odds that only appear on a relationship could be affecting your score without even realizing it.

A full one-third of your score depends on whether you pay your creditors on time. So, make sure you pay all your bills by their due dates, including rent/mortgage, utilities, doctor's bills, etc. Keep documentation (such as checks or cancelled receipts) to be able to prove that you have done the punctuality of payments.

The Fair Isaac Corporation, which calculates FICO scores, recommends signing up for payment notices if the lender makes them available. Another approach is to create automatic drafts from your bank account.

Pick up a payment order

When using your cards, try to pay them off as soon as you can (you do not need to wait for the instruction in the mail, but you can pay online at any time).

Do not open too many accounts

If you shop at that store, it can often be worth getting your card; otherwise, resist the temptation. What is more, every time you apply for credit the potential lender will check your score. Whenever the credit is selected, other potential lenders worry about the additional debt that they can take on. Sometimes, the act of opening a new account, or even applying for one, can lower the score; have a lot of recent inquiries about your credit report dings your score temporarily. So do not ask for the card often if you want to increase your credit score.

Do not close credit cards

A good idea would be to keep three or four credit card accounts open but use only one or two of them; put away or cut the others. Once you have paid a card, however, keep the account open, even if you do not want to use it anymore. In closing, late accounts or those with a history of late payments can also help, as long as you have paid them in full. Because history is important if you decide to close a couple of accounts, close the most recent ones. Be sure to use these cards to make occasional purchases (so pay the bills in full), so the card company does not close the account due to inactivity.

Increase the credit limit

There is a way to increase your credit score that does not involve paying a debt or any of the other more traditional credit score tactics by increasing. Since credit scores are determined, in part, on the difference between the credit limit and the amount of credit used, ask for a higher credit limit. Your chances of increasing it are probably better than you think. Of those applying for a higher credit limit, 8 out of 10 have been approved, according to a recent money survey. While it helps to be over 30, there is a good chance for all adults. To prevent the credit decreased with the request for a higher limit, to ask for the highest credit line increase that does not trigger what is called a difficult request.

By increasing the credit limit, the differential between the amount you are allowed to borrow and the amount you actually make is automatically increased. The larger the spread, the higher the credit score.

The credit utilization report

This spread, known as the credit utilization ratio, is expressed as a percentage. For example, if the limit on the MasterCard is $ 5,000 and you have a budget of $ 4,000, the usage ratio is 80%. If you request a credit line increase and the limit goes up to $ 10,000, suddenly your use is only 40%.

Obviously, the higher the percentage, the worse you look. Experts have long said that using 30% of available credit is a good way to keep your credit score high. More recently, this recommendation has been reduced to 20%. In the $ 5000 MasterCard limit example above, 30% usage would represent a $ 1,500 balance. Increasing the credit limit from $ 5,000 to $ 10,000 would allow a $ 3,000 balance and still maintain 30% utilization. This is also the reason why you should not close your accounts, which will increase the percentage of total available credit that you are using - and which will reduce your score.

Negotiate a lower interest rate

However, the key to this strategy is getting more credit, but no longer using credit. In other words, if the limit goes up to $ 1,000, do not go out and half responsible for it. Think of the push as a way to save money when applying for a car loan, home loan or another form of long-term debt where a high credit score will probably lead to big savings through a rate of lower interest.

Chapter 13. Credit Scoring Myth

For a large portion of credit scoring's history, by far, most of the people engaged with loaning decisions pretty much needed to think about what hurt or helped a score. Makers of scoring formulas would not like to uncover much about how the models functioned, for dread that contenders would take their thoughts or that consumers would make sense of how to beat the framework. Luckily, today we discover much increasingly about credit scoring—however, not every person has stayed aware of the latest knowledge. Mortgage intermediaries, loan officials, credit agency agents, credit guides, and the media, among others, continue to spread outdated and out and out bogus information. Following up on their terrible guidance can put your score and your accounts at critical risk.

Here are probably the most widely recognized fantasies.

Myth 1: Closing Credit Accounts Will Help Your Score

This one sounds sensible, particularly when a mortgage merchant discloses to you that lenders are suspicious of people who have heaps of unused credit accessible to them. All what’s you, all things considered, from hurrying out and charging up a tempest? Obviously, looking at the situation objectively, what's shielded you from piling on huge balances before now? If you've been responsible with credit before, you're probably going to continue to be responsible later. That is the essential standard behind credit scoring: Its rewards practices that show moderate, responsible utilization of credit after some time, because those propensities are probably going to continue.

The score likewise rebuffs conduct that is not all that responsible, for example, applying for a lot of credit you don't require. Numerous people with high credit scores locates that one of only a handful hardly any detriments for them is the number of credit accounts recorded on their reports. At the point when they go to get their credit scores, they're informed that one reason their score isn't considerably higher is that they have "too many open accounts." Many mistakenly expect they can "fix" this issue by closing accounts. In any case, after you've opened the accounts, you've done the damage. You can't fix it by closing the account. You can, however, make matters more awful.

Myth 2: You Can Increase Your Score by Asking Your Credit Card Company to Lower Your Limits

This one is a minor departure from the possibility that decreasing your accessible credit by one way or another enables your score by making you to appear to be less risky to lenders. By and by, it's missing the goal. Narrowing the difference between the credit you use and the credit you have accessible to you can negatively affect your score. It doesn't make a difference that you requested the decrease; the FICO formula doesn't recognize lower limits that you mentioned and lower limits forced by a creditor. All it sees is less difference between your balances and your limits, and that is not good. If that, you need to enable your score, to handle the issue from the opposite end: by paying down your debt. Expanding the gap between your balance and your credit limit positively affects your score.

Myth 3: You Need to Pay Interest to Obtain a Good Credit Score

This is the precise inverse of the past myth, and it's similarly as misinformed. It is not necessary for you to carry a balance on your credit cards and pay interest to have a good score. As you've perused a few times as of now, your credit reports—and subsequently the FICO formula—make no differentiation between balances you carry month to month and balances that you pay off. Savvy consumers don't carry credit card balances under any circumstances, and not to improve their scores. Presently, the facts confirm that to get the highest FICO scores, you must have both revolving accounts, for example, credit cards, and instalment loans, for example, a mortgage or car loan. What's more, except for those 0 per cent rates used to drive auto deals after Sept. 11, most instalment loans require paying interest.

Yet, here's a news streak: You don't have to have the highest score to get good credit. Any score more than 720 or so will get you the best rates and terms with numerous lenders. A few, particularly auto and home value lenders, save their best bargains for those with scores more than 760. You don't must have an 850, or even 800 score, to get incredible arrangements. In case you're attempting to improve a fair score, a little, reasonable instalment loan can help—if you can get affirmed for it and pay it off on time. However, some way or another, there's no motivation to stray into the red and pay interest.

Myth 4: Your Closed Accounts Should Indicate "Closed by Consumer," Or They Will Hurt Your Score

The hypothesis behind this myth is that lenders will see a closed account on your credit report and, if not educated generally, will accept that a nauseated creditor cut you off because you botched in some way or another. Obviously, as you most likely are aware at this point, numerous lenders never observe your real report. They're simply taking a gander at your credit score, which couldn't care less who closed a credit card. Fair Isaac figures that if a lender closes your account, it's either for dormancy or because you defaulted. If that you defaulted, that will be sufficiently archived in the account's history. If it makes you feel better to contact the bureaus and guarantee that accounts you closed are recorded as "closed by consumer," by all methods do as such. However, it won't make any distinction to your credit score.

Myth 5: Credit Counselling Is Way Worse Than Bankruptcy

Sometimes this is expressed as "credit advising is as awful as bankruptcy" or "credit directing is as terrible as bankruptcy." None of these statements is valid. A bankruptcy recording is the single most noticeably terrible thing you can do to your credit score. On the other hand, the current FICO formula totally ignores any reference to credit guiding that may be on your credit report. Credit guiding is treated as an impartial factor, neither aiding nor hurting your score. Credit guides, if you're inexperienced with the term, have practical experience in arranging lower interest rates and also working out payment plans for debtors that may some way or another file for bankruptcy. Although credit advisors may consolidate the consumer's bills into one monthly payment, they don't give loans—as debt consolidators do—or guarantee to wipe out or settle debts for not exactly the chief amount you owe.

The fact that credit guiding itself won't affect your score doesn't mean, notwithstanding, that enrolling in a credit advisor's debt management plan will leave your credit sound. A few lenders will report you as late only for enrolling in a debt management plan. Their thinking is that you're not paying them what you initially owed, so you ought to need to endure some agony. That is not, by any means, the only way you could be reported late. Not all credit instructors are made equivalent, and some have been blamed for retaining consumer payments that were proposed for creditors.

Chapter 14. How Credit System Works

In a nutshell, the entire credit system constitutes the credit bureaus, the creditors and you. Creditors are the companies you access credit from while the credit bureaus collect credit data from past and current creditors and compile it into reports, which are modelled in the form of credit profiles for each credit consumer, after which they sell these reports to creditors so that they can make various decisions.

The creditors use the data they obtain from credit bureaus to determine how much they will charge you for borrowing and the amount of penalties they should charge you for defaulting. Whenever a creditor needs credit profiles of people that have a certain credit score, they buy that information from the credit bureaus. This helps them to target their products and services since they will then send emails to those in that list enticing them to buy or use their products and services. It is believed that most of these companies go after those that have a low score. This will allow them to have a chance at making a greater profit and pulling out as much money as possible from these people's pockets.

The credit system consists of three parties namely you, the creditors, and the credit bureaus.

If a creditor needs a report of credit consumers who have a specific credit score, they can then buy the credit profiles from the credit bureaus thus making it easy to target products and services appropriately. They (creditors) will send you enticing information on offers that you should buy.

Subprime credit data is the best-selling for the different credit reporting agencies. Therefore, if you have a subprime credit rating. You are likely to be getting countless email solicitations for you to apply to different credit cards. The reasoning for this is straight forward. With a subprime credit rating, you are going to be charged more for accessing credit. This simply means that the lenders will make more money from you. If you have excellent credit rating, you are low risk and lenders charge you less for accessing credit, which means that they make less money when they advance your credit. In other terms, lenders will want to prey on you if you have bad credit because they are certain that they will make more money in the end. Even if you are to default, you are likely to have paid more money than someone who has good credit! Subprime data is such a hot selling product that the credit reporting agencies charge more for it; it is in high demand! This can be translated to mean that the creditors and credit bureaus don't care about you having good credit. In any case, if your credit rating is bad, they will charge you more! Do you know that over 90 per cent of credit reports have been proven to have inaccurate, unverifiable, and erroneous entries?

Well, now you know why your credit score is always becoming bad even with all your effort. These companies are in it for profit. They will even overlook when erroneous entries are posted in your report. In any case, they have convinced us to think that the reports are the gospel truth when they are nowhere close to that. So, in simple terms, these 2 players in the credit system can only be compelled by the law to put things in order. They have no interest in you having perfect credit because they all make more money if you have bad credit.

If you are in this group of credit consumers, you will get the most enticing offers and email solicitations to apply for credit cards. The reason is simple, as was mentioned, when your credit score isn't so good, the creditors will charge more for advancing your credit, which means that they make more money. In financial terms, creditors address their exposure to credit risk through charging more for credit. If you have the capacity to pay the right amount on time this will cause them to lose out on a substantial amount of profit. They will not be satisfied with what they receive and will want more out of their customers. They might not directly refuse you credit but will not be particularly interested in giving you money. They will be waiting for someone with bad credit to walk in. When you have poor credit, you might be paying up to three times what you would pay were you to have a perfect credit score.

So, the companies will expressly go after those that have a bad score and will put in all possible effort to trap them. As you can see, creditors will be inclined to prey on those with sub-prime credit score for the simple reason that they will make more money from them even if they were to default as they will have made money already! So, there is a lot of planning that they do just to fill up their pockets.

It should not surprise you that these companies work hand in hand. It takes effort from both ends for their schemes to work and they will ensure that they are on the same page. They will come up with plans that will benefit both and cause each to make a large profit at the expense of the customer. Imagine trying to cheat millions of customers on a yearly basis, it is a Herculean task and will require the company to be as prepared as possible to pull it off with ease. For this reason, they will join hands and make sure each one cuts into the profit.

Apart from these 2, there will be some third parties who will work to help these credit companies. These can be outsourced companies or independent ones looking to hook up with the credit companies and trying to make money for themselves. These will have the exclusive job of looking for people that have not checked their records for some time and determine to get them on board. They will put in a lot of effort to catch these people's fancy and once they trap them, they will direct them to the credit company and get them to pay for their services.

To prove that your bad credit history records are a best seller for credit reporting agencies, do you know that they will even charge more to credit providers to access such information. That's right, they will pay up a little extra just to find those that have a bad credit and start bombarding them with emails that ask them to apply for credit at their place. This means that none of these parties has any specific interest to have the information in your credit report reported accurately.

Do you know that only a small percentage of people file disputes for such items despite over 90 per cent of credit reports having been found to have erroneous, unverifiable and inaccurate entries? Many will not wish to go through the pain of proving themselves right. This allows the companies to have a long leash and they will not back away from exploiting these people. The companies have several good field days owing to such ignorance on the part of the customers.

The credit companies will be determined to report your bad credit and this means that some of them will even let such entries be included in your credit report for the simple reason that so few of us have the guts to challenge entries in the credit report even if they are incorrect, unverifiable and erroneous. They will know who exactly will not challenge it just by looking at your credit history. They will not have an interest in catering to those that might take up a dispute. They will employ people to especially look for those customers that have a bad score and those that look most likely to remain mum about errors in their reports.

The 2 other players in the credit system (the creditors and the credit reporting agencies) are in it to make the most money from you directly or indirectly so counting on them to help you make things right should be out of the question. The more screwed up your credit score is, the more money there is to be made by the credit reporting agencies and the creditors. That is, the lower the score, the better their prospects to charge you a bomb.

So, when you file a dispute, the creditors and the credit reporting agencies will only update the data - not because they have any interest in your welfare - but because they don't have an option given to them and they are under legal obligation to act in accordance with the law. They will not expressly pursue your cause and, in fact, despite your efforts to fix your bad score, they will try and remain ignorant of it and make things worse for you. They will go to any lengths just to make sure that you have no chance of fixing your score despite none of it being your fault.

This is the exact reason why there are hundreds, probably thousands, of people who despise credit card companies. They will not stop at anything and fall to the absolute lows just to make a few extra dollars. Many of these companies will have a bad reputation and yet find easy prey for themselves. They will know how exactly they can target the customers and get them to subscribe to their card. Once the person is trapped, they will not stop until they fulfil their desire to make as much money as possible. The poor customer will be trapped and will have to surrender to the demands of the vicious company.

Every day, there are hundreds of innocent customers who fall for this trick and do not put in the effort to check their credit reports. But it is important for every person to thoroughly go through their report and look for any erroneous and wrong entries that may be causing them their low scores.

Now that you understand that only yourself is on your side on matters pertaining the accuracy of the credit report, how do you know how your credit score affects your ability to borrow? It is apparent that your score is the most vital element in your report and something that needs to be investigated carefully. But what is this score and what are its parameters? How do you know that your score is good, average or bad?

Of course the report doesn't state that a certain amount is bad, so understanding what benchmarks the lenders are going to use in categorizing you as good (perfect), average (sub-prime) and bad will be very helpful so that you know what to expect when you see that number on your credit report.

Credit Repair

Introduction

You're here because you want to know how credit repair works. We're not going to beat around the bush with you. Credit repair isn't easy work and it won't be a quick process either. You've done the preliminary legwork in trying to get your finances back in order by setting financial targets, creating a schedule, seeking ways to save money, and requesting a copy of your credit report. Now that you have a copy of your credit report from one of the three credit reporting agencies, it's time to roll up your sleeves and fix the misleading details on your credit report.

What Is Credit Repair and How Does It Work?

Credit repair is the method of repairing credit status that has degraded due to a number of factors. It could be as simple as disputing the details to improve your credit score. Another type of credit repair is to address financial issues such as budgeting and begin to address concerns.

Significant Points to consider

- Credit repair is the method of raising or repairing one's credit score.

- Paying a company to contact the credit bureau and point out something in your report that is misleading or wrong, and demanding that it be deleted, is another choice for credit repair.

How Credit Repair Works

While businesses claim to be able to clean up bad credit reports, doing so takes time and effort. The details cannot be removed by a third party. Specifics that are wrong or misrepresented may be challenged. If their credit reports contain inaccurate or incomplete information, they can file a dispute. Fixing and repairing credit may have a greater impact on credit usage and action than correcting such advice or catching fraudulent trades on one's credit. This person's payment background may have an effect on their credit score. Taking steps to ensure that payments are made on time or to improve the payment program for unpaid credit can have a negative effect on their credit score. The total amount of credit you have could be a factor. For example, if someone is knowingly using large amounts of credit available to them, even if they are making minimum payments on time, the size of their debt may have a negative impact on their credit score. The issue is that their liquidity can be influenced by their debt. They could see results if they took action to reduce their debt.

Creditors Can Help

If you have a long-standing account with a creditor, you can also contact them directly to clarify the mistake on your credit report. Request that they write you a letter containing the email and the correction. In addition, request that they notify each credit reporting agency that has received this incorrect entry in order to correct it.

Create a copy of the letter and attach it to the letter of dispute you send after the creditor receives a copy. Submit it to the credit reporting service and ask them to update their records. The credit reporting agency will send you a new credit report after it is done.

Chapter 1. Is Credit Repair Bad and Ethical?

Beware, not all credit repair companies are ethical. Do not fall for scams that promise they can take a bad credit record and turn it around overnight. Or that guarantee they can "force" the credit bureaus to remove all negative (but accurate) information from your credit file immediately. It takes time and your cooperation to improve your credit. Trust me when I tell you that a credit repair company cannot push around the large credit bureaus. Never mind order them to do things like immediately remove foreclosures or missed payments from the records of their client's. Inaccurate information can be easily fixed. However, removing accurate negative information takes a plan and is rarely done overnight. That usually requires filing official disputes, and careful negotiations with your creditors.

Some credit repair companies not only misrepresent what they can do for you, but also practice illegal or fraudulent ways of trying to improve your credit. Often, they will reorganize as a non-profit to get around state and federal laws that govern the industry. If you are desperate enough, you may be tempted to risk some of these illegal actions, but we would not recommend it. People have lost hundreds, and in some cases thousands of dollars to credit repair scams.

The Warning Signs When Choosing a Credit Repair Company

-They recommend that you do not contact credit bureaus directly.

-They do not disclose your legal rights or what you can do yourself.

-They want you to pay upfront based on their verbal promises before they do any work. They can only charge you after they have completed the services they contracted for.

-They suggest unethical or illegal actions such as making false statements on a loan application, misrepresenting your social security number, or obtaining an EIN number under false pretensions. The use of these tactics could constitute general fraud, civil fraud, mail fraud, wire fraud, and get you into a lot of trouble.

The Disputing Process

The first thing you need to know is that all three credit reporting agencies have to contest the inaccurate information independently. The disputed appearance may be on all three credit reports or may not. Keep in mind that customers may not belong to all credit reporting agencies. This is why you will see that on one list some of the investors are not on the others.

Even though all three credit reporting agencies have the same information, this does not mean that if an item comes out of one credit report it will come out of the others. No promise is provided what the outcome will be. That is why you have to refute any inaccurate information about each particular article.

They can use their appeal forms when disputing with credit reporting agencies, write your own message, or challenge the item online on their Website. If you decide to dispute by letter-writing, simply state the facts in a simple, concise or two sentences. If you choose to write a personalized message, you can also use the same answers as appropriate. Sample answers would be:

- This is not my account.
- This was not late as indicated.
- This was not charged off.
- This was paid off in full as agreed.
- This was not a collection account.
- This is not my bankruptcy as indicated.
- This is not my tax lien as indicated.
- This is not my judgment as indicated.

If you have found more than four entries on your credit report that you need to dispute, do not dispute everything in one letter. Whether you are writing a letter, filling out their form or answering via the Internet, break your disputes. You send or go back every 30 days to the website of the credit reporting agency and challenge up to four more things. On submitting each address, expect to receive a revised credit report about 45 days after you send your letter or disagreement online. If your new credit report has not been issued before it is time to appeal the second time, go ahead and mail your second letter or challenge online instead.

Once all the grievance letters have been mailed or posted to their website and all the revised credit reports have been received, check whether products have been omitted or incomplete. If you need to do the procedure again for the remaining items, space 120 days from your most recent update for another disputes.

What you should not do:

- Alter your identity or try to change it.
- The story is fictional.
- Check any information which is 100% correct.

What you should do:

- Read your emails, should you decide to send them to us? If a letter looks legitimate, credit reporting agencies will believe it has been written by a credit repair service, and they will not investigate the dispute.
- Use your original letterhead (if you do have one).
- Use the appeal form included with the credit report by the credit reporting agency, if you want.

- Provide some evidence suggesting the wrong entry is erroneous.

- Include the identification number for all communications listed on the credit report.

Spotting Possible Identity Theft

Checking your credit report could also spot potential identity theft. That is why you should inquire at least once a year or every six months for a copy of your credit report.

Things to look for would be:

- Names of accounts and figures that you do not know.

- You do not remember filling out loan applications.

- Addresses you did not live in.

- Poor bosses or tenants' enquiries you do not know.

Credit Rescoring

Rapid rescoring is an expedited way of fixing anomalies in the credit file of a customer. A fast rescore dispute process works through borrowers and mortgage brokers, a number of approved registry credit reporting companies, and credit reporting agencies.

If you are a creditor applying for a rescore on your credit report, you would need to provide detailed documents that would be sent to the collateral agencies that are working on your case. Cash registry is the system used by cash grantors. The data archive gathers the records from the three main credit reporting agencies and has to check the consumer's initial information for a rescore. Once the verification is entered into the program of the repository a new score will be produced.

The downside of a fast rescore is that you save money without having to contend individually with a credit reporting agency that may take longer than 30 days to complete an audit. If the sale of a house or lease depends on your credit score, and you are in a time crunch, the best solution is to easily rescore.

First Step in Actually Repairing Your Credit

Write letters to the agencies with the correct but bad items you have encountered and your reasoning for which you think they should be taken off your credit report. The most important thing when writing these letters and when making any type of contact with the people at the credit report agencies is to keep communication very polite and professional. The more pleasant and prepared you are, the more you increase the chances of them helping you repair your credit. Sign and date your letters and try to write them by hand.

Contact with the Creditor

At this point, you have to write another letter, this time to the creditor. You can continue claiming that the negative information is wrong but be warned that they will not believe you if you do not provide solid proof to back up your claim. If you do not think you can muster up that proof in order to make a good case for re-establishing your good credit.

Chapter 2. Secrets Steps of Credit Repair

Step 1: Know your credit score

First things first, see what your credit score is and check your credit report. Most people will tell you that you can check your credit report for free once a year by visiting www.AnnualCreditReport.com. Also, if you are trying to fix your credit score, you will need to check your report at least once a month, not once a year. Other people might also direct you to sources that charge you for checking your credit score or that hurt your credit score every time you check it. Do not do that.

Following is a list of FREE resources where you can check your credit score without having to worry about it costing a thing or hurting your credit:

- www.creditkarma.com – use this site when fixing your credit score. The site provides free credit reports and scores from Equifax and Transunion that are updated every week.
- www.creditsesame.com - Same as credit karma but updates every month instead of week. It gives you a free credit score, but not a free credit report.
- www.quizzle.com - offers a free credit report and score every 3 months.

- www.credit.com - You get two free credit reports and your score is updated once a month.
- www.wallethub.com - gives daily updates to its free credit scores and reports. There are some more websites out there, but these are the most popular.

Once you have signed up with one of these sites and checked your credit score, it is time to analyze your credit report for errors.

Step 2: Thoroughly scan your credit report

Everyone has three credit reports: one from Experian, one from Equifax, and one from Transunion. These are the three big credit bureaus.

Once you get your free report, thoroughly go over it. Is everything correct? Remember, it is actually quite common for mistakes to be on your credit report. It is very important for you to highlight any errors these should be removed from your report, which will increase your credit score

When going through record put these in mind. Are all of my accounts listed? Is my personal information correct? Are all missed and/or late payments correctly listed? Is there anything I do not recognize? Are there still accounts listed that are decades-old? Go over every single thing.

Step 3: Fixing errors on your credit report

First, go over all missed/late payments. Check if you recognize it. If not, dispute it. Have you paid it already? Dispute it. Is the payment more than 7 years old? Dispute it. Other people are inclined to tell you that you need to pay your missed payments and collections so you can just be done with it.

Then check the inquires done on your credit. Dispute any incorrect or unauthorized inquires. Same goes for collections and public records. This is one of the secrets of fixing bad credit. Before disputing, make sure that you are not disputing something that is positively influencing your credit score. Only dispute personal information, credit inquiries, charge offs, collections, bankruptcies, foreclosures, repossessions, tax liens, judgments and others.

But how exactly do you dispute a charge? For every error, you need to dispute it by all three credit bureaus. I suggest writing them a letter via postal mail, but nowadays you can also dispute charges online. The problem with filing a dispute online is that oftentimes, you agree to not being able to sue them if the charge is not removed. You limit your rights, giving you less control and making the process less effective.

Also, do not dispute via phone. You need evidence and records of your dispute. You can easily find a sample letter which you can send to the credit bureaus. All the credit bureaus also have their own dispute letter form, just check their website. Print and mail the dispute letter along with ID and proof of address.

Step 4: Passed Payment History

Your past payment history has the biggest impact. Fix any late payments and avoid late payments in the future. What you can do is setting up payment due alerts and becoming more organized. If the due dates are inconsistent with the dates you get paid, talk with your bank or lender to change the payment date. If you get paid at the end of every month, change your due date to the end of every month too. If fixing any late payments is hard, request the issuer or lender if they can forgive the charge. Tell them that you were out on vacation, the check got lost via the mail, or you did not get notice of the bill and did not know it existed. Some issuers, especially credit card issuers, are pretty soft-hearted if you have had a strong track record of making payments in the past. What is worse than having a bad payment history, is having no payment history. If you have no payment history, try getting a secured credit card and making on-time payments in order to build up a healthy payment history. Really try to pay your bills on time in the future.

Step 5: Debt-to-Credit Ratio

Keep the balances low. Avoid maxing out. You could make all your payments on time, but it is also essential to keep your balance low when it comes to your credit card, or any revolving credit account for that matter. Credit cards are the main weight of debt-ratio rates, so if you do not have a credit card, definitely get one. To figure out your credit card's debt-ratio, divide your credit card balance by your available credit line. So if you spent $200 out of your $1000 credit line, that's 200/1000=0.2, which is 20%. This is good. FICO recommends a debt-to-credit ratio to be under 30%. If your debt-to-credit ratio is at or above 30%, decrease your spending or increase your credit line, your bank will likely agree to increasing your credit line.

Step 6: Negotiate your existing accounts

If you have open accounts that are severely delinquent, showing late payments or slow payments contact the creditor(s) and try to negotiate a new payment arrangement.

- Ask for more time to pay-off the loan; consider this, if you have a 36 months term loan ask if it can be extended to 42 months
- Ask for a lower interest rate?
- Ask what are your options?
- You can do this yourself without the help of those companies and organizations that try to put you on a special payment plan charging lots of money to do something you can do for yourself. This is extra money that can be used to pay off some of that debt. Simply explain to the creditor(s) you are having financial difficulties, below are some typical hardships:
- going through a divorce
- getting sick and being under-insured or no medical insurance
- death of a close relative (parent, sibling, spouse, child)
- losing a job or job cutting back on hours

- a major car repairs (replace engine/transmission)
- car accident
- becoming disabled
- a run of bad luck, etcetera

Remember to notate your schedule on all the progress you have made negotiating your payoffs.

Chapter 3. Strategies to Repair your Credit Score

Pay to Delete Strategy

If you have derogatory items in your credit report, you can opt to pay the unpaid credit balance only if the creditor agrees to delete the items from your credit report. As I already mentioned, don't agree for a $0 balance appearing on your credit report since this taints your reputation. This will ultimately improve your rating. Actually, the idea is to ensure that whatever amount you agree to pay doesn't show up as your last date of activity. If the creditor only cares about their money, why should they bother telling the world that you have finally paid?

In most instances, the creditors often write off debts within just 2 years of constant defaulting after which this information is sold in bulk to a collection company for some pennies of a dollar. This means that the collection companies will even be just fine if you even pay a fraction of what you ought to pay. Whatever you pay, they will still make money! This makes them open to negotiations such as pay to delete since they have nothing to lose anyway.

Chapter 4. Therefore, only use the pay to delete approach at this level and not any other. Actually, the only other way around it for the collection company is a judgment, which can be costly, so you have some advantage here.

Chapter 5. Additionally, use this strategy when new negative items start showing up in your report that could hurt your reputation as a credit consumer.

Chapter 6. Also, since the creditors will often sell the same information to multiple collection companies, you might probably start noting the same debt being reported by several companies; use pay to delete to get them off your report.

Chapter 7. You can also use this strategy if you have not been successful in getting items off your credit report using other methods. This is opting to go the dispute way might only make the process cyclic, which will be cumbersome, tiresome and frustrating; you don't want to get into this cycle.

Now that you know when to use this method, understanding how the entire process works is very critical. To start with, ensure that you get an acceptance in writing if they agree to your times; don't pay without the letter! After you agree, allow about 45 days for next credit report to be availed to you by your credit monitoring service. These companies have the legal power to initiate the deletion process so don't accept anything less such as updating the balance; it is either a deletion or nothing. Don't worry if one company seems not to agree with your terms since another one will probably show up and will gladly take the offer.

In any case, what do they have to gain when they keep your debt when you are willing to pay? Remember that the records will just be in your records for 7 years so since 2 years are already past, these companies have no choice otherwise you can simply let the 7 years to pass! However, don't use this as an excuse for not paying your debts since the creditors can sue you to compel you to pay outstanding amounts. The aim of this process is to ensure that whatever bad experience you have with one creditor doesn't make the others to make unfavorable decisions on your part.

NOTE: don't be overly aggressive with creditors who have a lot to lose in the process especially the recent creditors since they can probably sue you. Your goal is to only be aggressive with creditors that are barred by the statute of limitation from suing you in court. You don't want to find yourself in legal trouble to add to your existing problems. Try and remain as smart as possible and make all the right moves to help you repair your credit at the earliest.

Pay to delete isn't the only option available to you; you can use other strategies to repair your credit.

Check for FDCPA (Fair Debt Collection Practices Act) Violations

The law is very clear on what collection agencies can do and what they cannot do as far as debt collection is concerned. For instance:

- They should not call you more than once in a day unless they can prove that it was accidentally dialed by their automated systems.
- They cannot call you before 8.00.am or after 9.00pm.
- They cannot threaten, belittle or yell at you to make you pay any outstanding debts.
- They cannot tell anyone else other than your spouse why they are contacting you.
- The best way to go about this is to let them know that you are recording all their calls.

- They cannot take more money from your account than you have authorized if they do an ACH.
- They are also not allowed to send you collection letters if you have already sent them a cease and desist order.

If you can prove that collection companies are in violation of the laws, you should file a complaint with the company then have your lawyer send proof indicating the violations; you can then request that any outstanding debt be forgiven. You need to understand that the law is on your side in such circumstances; actually, if the violations are major, the collection companies could be forced to pay fines of up to $10,000 for these violations.

So, if your debt is significantly lower than this, you could be on your way to having your debt cleared since these companies would rather pay your debt than pay the fine.

Look for Errors on your Credit Reports

Your credit report should be free of errors. Even the slightest thing as reporting the wrong date of last activity on your credit report is enough to damage your credit. If the write off date is different from what has been reported, you can dispute the entry to have it corrected to reflect that actual status of your credit. However, keep in mind that the credit bureaus will in most instances confirm that the negative entry is correct even if this is not the case, which means that they will not remove the erroneous item.

You must put in efforts to get them on the right track. To get them to comply, you have to inform them that the law requires them to have preponderance of their systems in place to ensure that these errors do not arise. Therefore, the mere fact of confirming the initial error is not enough. Inform them about the Notice (Summons) and complaint to let them understand that you are serious about the matter. Once they have an idea of your stance, they will put in efforts to do the right thing. The thing is; the bureaus don't want any case to go to court since this could ultimately provide proof that their systems are weak or flawed, which means that they will probably be in some bigger problems.

So try and drive a strong point across so that they understand you mean business. Mere exchange of emails will not do and you must send them details on how strong your case will be. This will make them understand their position and they will decide to help you to avoid going to court. This will, in turn, work to your advantage in making them to dig deeper into the issue. However, this method will only work if you are certain that an error was actually made. You will also require proof for it and cannot simply state that there was an error.

Request Proof of the Original Debt

If you are certain that the credit card has been written off for late payment, it is highly likely that the carriers (Capital One and Citibank) cannot find the original billing statements within 30 days, which they are required by the law to respond. This in effect allows you to have whatever entry you have disputed removed from the credit report as if it never happened.

Another handy approach is to request for the original contract that you signed to be provided to prove that you actually opened that particular credit card in the first instance. As you do this, don't just ask for "verification" since this just prompts the collection agency to "verify" that they actually received a request for collection on an account that has your name on it. Pay the Original Creditor

When your debt is sold to collection agencies, you will probably risk having new items showing up on your credit report, which can further hurt your credit rating.

However, you can stop that by sending a check with the full payment of any outstanding amount to the original creditor after which you just send a proof of payment to that collection agency and any other then request them to delete any derogatory items they have reported from your credit report.

It is always a good idea to be in direct contact with your creditor or creditors. In fact, many of these agencies will be fully equipped to cheat you and will follow through on plans to have your report show bad credit scores. It is up to you to try and remove these "middlemen" and do the payment yourself. You could also enter into an agreement to pay a portion of the money to the creditor as full payment for the sum (the pay to delete strategy).

Under the federal law, if the original creditor accepts any payment as full payment for any outstanding debt, the collection agency has to remove whatever they have reported. This will only work if the original creditor accepts the payment; it is possible for some of the checks you pay to the original creditor to be returned to you.

How to remove your Debt

Remember that you need to focus on paying off all your debts at the earliest. You cannot waste any more time and must try and finish them off to have a good score. Let us now look at the things that you need to do to pay off your debts on time.

You can pay off your debts in one of the two methods that are made available viz. the first one being the avalanche method and the second being the snowball method. Each type has its own advantages and disadvantages. You need to look at whatever fits your budget best and go for it without wasting any more time. If you think you have enough money saved up then choose the avalanche method but if you have very little then chose the snowballing method. Apart from these, if you have enough money to pay everything all together then you can choose that option as well.

Planning

Remember to always work with a plan. When you have everything planned out it will be easy for you to finish your task. Start by preparing a monthly budget by including your incomes and expenses and try and balance it out to remain with as much money at the end as possible. You need to add your debts to the expenses column and this will help you pay them on time. When you are left with a surplus, you can use it to open a separate "debt repayment" account and add in the money there. Once you have a substantial amount, you can use it to pay off all your debts.

Organizing

Mere planning will not suffice and you need to be as organized as possible. You must have everything in place to help you operate smoothly. Try having a different account for each of your debts so that money automatically gets transferred every month. You must also have a set monthly budget for your expenses. You must not use any more money than what you have assigned. When you are organized, you will feel that your life is easy and there are not many obstacles standing in your way.

Contact

The next step is to contact your creditors. This means that you get in touch with them and assure them that you are going to pay your debts on time. Many times, it pays to develop a good rapport with your creditors. But don't push it and remain within your limits. You need to develop a rapport and not a close friendship with them. You need to win over their trust and make them like your determination. Remain in touch with them and update them on your every move to repay their debts on time. After a while, the informality between the two of you will start to reduce.

Negotiate

When you have struck a good rapport, you can decide to ask for a small rebate in your debt or negotiate the rate of interest that you have to pay. This might not be possible with all creditors such as banks but you can try your luck with moneylenders and other non-commercial lenders. Once they are happy with your timely debt repayments they might decide to reduce the interest rate by a little. But don't expect them to waive off your loan as nobody will be willing to do that. You can ask them if you can pay a little less for the last few installments and count that as your rebate.

Secured credit card

When you are trying to pay off all your debts at the earliest, you must not use your credit card excessively. Your credit score will plummet and so, it is best that you give up on these. There are alternatives to credit cards that you can consider. Debit cards are a great idea as you will only draw money from your own account when you use these. Buy if you want to have the feel of a credit card then you can opt for a secured credit card. These are issued by your bank and they will be linked to your account. You will have to add money to this account and there will be a limit on how much you can draw in a month. There will be no interest levied on the amount and you must add back the money that you withdrew within a specified period of time to help the account remain active.

Family

Sometimes, if there is a lot of debt then you can consider borrowing some money from your relatives. When you do so, you will be able to pay off a debt easily. Your family members might not charge you a high rate of interest and it might be within your budget. You can consider asking your dad or your uncle or anybody who is in a position to pay you the amount at the earliest. You need not stress over paying the sum back to them and can do it leisurely and at your own pace.

Life insurance

It is also possible for you to borrow money from your life insurance policy. You can ask for a certain amount that you promise to pay back within a specified period of time. There is no interest as such that will be levied on this sum and you can repay it after a few years' time. Once you repay your debt and give back to your insurance company then you will truly be free and your credit score will start to rise high.

Bank borrowing

It pays to have everything unified to make for easy payments. This means that you can borrow a certain amount from your bank and pay off all your creditors in bulk. You can then pay only to your bank to settle your debts. This will make it easier for you as you have to pay to only one institution. The rate of interest might also be low and that will help you save on a lot of money. The only disadvantage of this type is that, not many banks entertain this sort of borrowing. However, you can try your luck and approach two or more banks with a proposal.

Money savers

Every month, think of ways in which you can save on money. This can be by way of using coupons while shopping or making use of store credit to help save on the bill etc. You can also sell your old and unused stuff to make some money out of it. It is also a good idea to gift a service instead of a physical gift as this will further help you in saving money. Nevertheless, if you cannot gift a service every time then you can consider buying them in bulk after the holiday is over and store it to be gifted the next year. Cutting down on electricity, water and gas bills will also help you save money. It is also ideal for you to buy second hand goods for the time being and save further.

You can follow these steps to repay all your loans at the earliest and improve your credit score.

Chapter 4. Understanding FCRA and Section 609

When you are going about trying to fix your credit, it can often feel as though the deck is stacked against you, however, the truth of the matter is that there are several laws that can help you to even the odds when it comes to dealing with both creditors and credit bureaus.

FCRA: The FCRA does more than just provide you with a free credit report each year, it also regulates the various credit reporting organizations and helps to ensure that the information they gather on you is both accurate and fair. This means that if you see inaccurate information on your credit report, and report it to the relevant agency, they are legally required to look into the matter and resolve it, typically within 30 days. The same applies to agencies or organizations that generally add details to your credit report. Finally, if an organization that reviews your credit report decides to charge your more or declines to do business with you based on what they find in your report, they are legally obligated to let you know why and what report they found the negative information in.

While this won't help you with that particular lender, if the information is inaccurate you will at least know where to go to clear up the issue. Additionally, if you report an inaccuracy and the credit reporting agency ignores your request you can sue them to recover the damages or a minimum of $2,500. You may also be able to win an additional amount based on punitive damages and legal fees and any other associated costs. You must file legal proceedings within 5 years of when this occurs.

What Is Section 609? Is a 609 Dispute Letter Effective?

The first thing that we need to take a look at here when it comes to our credit scores is what Section 609 is really all about. This is going to be one of the best ways for you to get your credit score up, and outside of a little calling or sending out mail, you will not have to do as much to get it all done. Let's dive in now and see if we are able to learn a bit more about it.

The FCRA or the Fair Credit Reporting Act, is going to cover a lot of the aspects and the components of credit checking to make sure that it is able to maintain a reasonable amount of privacy and accuracy along the way. This agency is going to list out all of the responsibilities that credit reporting companies, and any credit bureaus, will have, and it also includes the rights of the consumer, which will be your rights in this situation. This Act is going to be the part that will govern how everything is going to work to ensure that all parties are treated in a fair manner.

This Act is going to limit the access that third-parties can have to your file. You personally have to go through and provide your consent before someone is able to go through and look at your credit score, whether it is a potential employer or another institution providing you with funding.

They are not able to get in and just look at it. Keep in mind that if you do not agree for them to take a look at the information, it is going to likely result in you not getting the funding that you want, because there are very few ways that the institution can fairly assess the risk that you pose to them in terms of creditworthiness.

There are several ways that a credit agency can go through and break or violate the FCRA, so this allows the consumer a way to protect themselves if that proves to be something that needs to happen.

Another thing to note about all of this is that the FCRA is going to be divided into sections. In particular, section 609 of the FCRA is going to deal with disclosure and is going to put all of the burdens of providing the right kind of documentation on the credit bureaus.

This may sound a little bit confusing, but it means that you may have debt or another negative item that is on your credit report, but there is a way to get around this without having to wait for years to get that to drop off your report or having to pay back a debt that you are not able to afford.

Keep in mind that this is not meant to be a method for you to take on a lot of debts that you can't afford and then just dump them. But on occasion, there could be a few that you are able to fight and get an instant boost to your credit score in the process.

You do not have to come up with a way of proving whether or not the item on the credit report is legitimate or not. Instead, that is up to the credit bureaus. And there are many cases where they are not able to do this. Whether they bought the debt and did not have the proper documentation, or there is something else that is wrong with it, the credit company may not be able to prove that you are the owner of it or that you owe on it at all. If this is the case, they have to remove the information from your credit report. When a bad debt is taken off, or even a collection is taken off, that does nothing but a lot of good for your overall score.

Some of Your Rights Under Section 609 and How You Can Use These to Your Advantage.

According to Section 609 of the Fair Credit Reporting Act, the credit bureaus are not allowed to list any credit agreements without verifying their validity first. The creditor is supposed to send a copy of the credit agreement for the bureaus to validate and keep in case there are any inquiries.

This is important because the bureaus generally skip this step. It is expensive and time consuming for them to verify all the information they receive. By law, the bureaus are required to provide proof that they have verified the information within thirty days. If they cannot provide proof of the original agreement or subsequent evidence of negative listings, and you can prove your identity, then they must remove the listing. It does not matter if the information is accurate or not. That is why it's important to monitor your credit.

To take advantage of this law, the first thing you need to do is to send a physical letter to the billing inquiries address that the creditor provides. If they turn down your request you are then allowed to ask for all the documentation saying why they turned you down.

A subset of this law is what is known as the Hidden Gem Law, this means you can dispute any transaction made within 100 miles of your home, or anywhere in your home state, which exceeds $50. If the debt collector breaks these rules or acts in other ways they are not allowed then you can file a private lawsuit and be recouped costs, fees and damages. What's more, you don't even need to prove damages and you will likely be awarded a minimum of $1,000.

Ways to Approach the Financial Institution

If the credit reporting agency is struggling to alter your report and you think the information is incomplete or wrong --you will want to take action. Below are a few suggestions that will assist you with your attempts.

Contact the Creditor Directly

Contacts the lender, which supplied the advice and demand it inform the credit. Request to Creditor composes your letter or to Eliminate. You can use inaccurate Information. You receive a letter from the lender and ought to be deleted from the credit history if, send a copy of the letter to the bureau that made the faulty report. If you contacted the Funding, it does not need to manage this dispute unless you supply the info. But since you think you also demonstrate a foundation for the belief, and the dispute wasn't properly researched should you increase your complaint, just like the president or CEO, the provider is very likely to reply. If the company cannot or won't help you in removing the info that is inaccurate, call the credit reporting agency.

Document another Dispute with the Credit Reporting Agency with More Information

If you have info backs up your claim, it is possible to submit a fresh dispute. Make sure to provide info. Should you dispute the mistake without giving any info to the bureau, it will determine that your dispute is frivolous, so the bureau does not need to inquire into the issue.

File a Complaint about the Credit Reporting Agency

You can file a complaint regarding a Credit reporting bureau together with the Consumer Financial Protection Bureau (CFPB). The CFPB attempt to have a response and will forward your complaint. In the event the CFPB believes another government agency will be able to assist you, it allows you to know and will forward your complaint.

File a Complaint Concerning the Creditor

If the lender supplied The erroneous or incomplete data fails to revise it or notify the credit reporting service of a correction (or even if it advises the credit reporting bureau of this alteration, but reports the incorrect information again after), you might file a complaint with the Federal Trade Commission (FTC). Or, if the lender is a big institution, you might file a complaint. The CFPB manages Types of agencies, and that means a complaint can document. If you are not sure which agency to contact, begin with CFPB or even the FTC, which will forward your complaint. Normally, you won't be represented by these government agencies. However, they could send an inquiry, and they may take action when there are complaints or proof of wrongdoing.

Complain for Your State Consumer Protection Agency

Some countries have to credit reporting lenders or bureaus furnishing information. File a complaint with the attorney general or consumer protection bureau of your state.

Consider Adding an Explanatory Statement for Your Credit Report

You've got the right Statement to your credit score. As soon as you submit a statement regarding the dispute using a credit reporting agency, the agency must include your statement--or a list of it. It might limit your announcement. In case the agency helps you in writing the excuse. There is not a term limit. Nonetheless, it is a fantastic idea to maintain the announcement shortly. In this way, the credit reporting agency is inclined to utilize your remark.

Chapter 5. Templates 609

Letter #1

(Initial Letter to Credit Bureau Disputing Items)

{Name of Bureau}

{Address}

{Date}

{Name on account}

{Report number}

To whom it may concern:

On {Date of Credit Report} I received a copy of my credit report which contains errors that are damaging to my credit score. I am requesting the following items be completely investigated as each account contains several mistakes.

{Creditor 1 / Account number}

{Creditor 2 / Account number}

{Creditor 3 / Account number}

Thank you in advance for your time. I understand that you need to check with the original creditors on these accounts and that you will make sure every detail is accurate. I also understand that under the Fair Credit Reporting Act you will need to complete your investigation within 30 days of receiving this letter. Once you are finished with your investigation, please send me a copy of my new credit report showing the changes. Looking forward to hear from you as I am actively looking for a new job and wouldn't want these mistakes on my credit report to stand in my way.

Sincerely,

{Your signature}

{Your Printed Name}

{Your Address}

{Your Phone Number}

{Your Social Security Number}

Attach a copy of the credit report showing which accounts you are disputing

Letter #2

(When you don't get a response from Letter #1)

{Name of Bureau}

{Address}

{Date}

{Name on account}

{Report number}

To whom it may concern:

On {Date of your first letter} I sent you a letter asking you to investigate several mistakes on my credit report. I've included a copy of my first letter and a copy of the report with the mistakes circled. The Fair Credit Reporting Act says I should only have to wait 30 days for the investigation to be finished. It has been more than 30 days and I still have not heard anything.

I'm guessing that since you have not responded that you were not able to verify the information on the mistaken accounts. Since it has been more than 30 days, please remove the mistakes from my credit report and send me a copy of my updated credit report. Also, as required by law, please send an updated copy of my credit report to anyone who requested a copy of my credit file in the past six months.

Looking forward to hear from you as I am actively looking for a new job and wouldn't want these mistakes on my credit report to stand in my way.

Sincerely,

{Your signature}

{Your Printed Name}

{Your Address}

{Your Phone Number}

{Your Social Security Number}

Attach a copy of the credit report showing which accounts you are disputing

Attach a copy of your original letter

Attach a copy of the registered letter receipts showing the date they received your original letter

Letter #3

(Request for removal of negative items from original creditor)

{Name of Creditor}

{Address}

{Date}

{Name on account}

To whom it may concern:

On {Date of Credit Report} I received a copy of my credit report which contains errors that are damaging to my credit score. I am requesting the following items be completely investigated as each account contains several mistakes.

{Description of item(s) you are disputing/account number(s)}

I have enclosed a duplicate of the credit report and have highlighted the account(s) in question.

Thank you in advance for your time. I understand that you need to check on these accounts and that you will make sure every detail is accurate. I also understand that under the Fair Credit Reporting Act you will need to complete your investigation within 30 days of receiving this letter. Once you are finished with your investigation, please alert all major credit bureaus where you have reported my information. Also, please send me a letter confirming the changes.

Looking forward to hear from you as I am actively looking for a new job and wouldn't want these mistakes on my credit report to stand in my way.

Sincerely,

{Your signature}

{Your Printed Name}

{Your Address}

{Your Phone Number}

{Your Social Security Number}

Attach a copy of the credit report showing which accounts you are disputing

Letter #4

(If you don't receive a response from Letter #3)

{Name of Creditor}

{Address}

{Date}

{Name on account}

To whom it may concern:

On {Date of your first letter} I sent you a letter asking you to investigate several mistakes on my credit report. I've included a copy of my first letter and a copy of the report with the mistakes circled. The Fair Credit Reporting Act says I should only have to wait 30 days for the investigation to be finished. It has been more than 30 days and I still have not heard anything.

I'm guessing that since you have not responded that you were not able to verify the information on the mistaken accounts. Since it has been more than 30 days, please immediately report the updated information to all major credit bureaus so they may update my credit report. Also, please send me a letter confirming these changes to the way you report my account.

Looking forward to hear from you as I am actively looking for a new job and wouldn't want these mistakes on my credit report to stand in my way.

Sincerely,

{Your signature}

{Your Printed Name}

{Your Address}

{Your Phone Number}

{Your Social Security Number}

Attach a copy of the credit report showing which accounts you are disputing

Attach a copy of your original letter

Attach a copy of the registered letter receipts showing the date they received your original letter

Letter #5

(If the Credit Bureau doesn't remove negative items disputed)

{Name of Credit Bureau}

{Address}

{Date}

{Name on account}

{Report number}

To whom it may concern:

On {Date of your first letter} I sent you a letter asking you to investigate several mistakes on my credit report. I've included a copy of my first letter and a copy of the report with the mistakes circled. According to your response you have chosen to leave these negative items on my credit report adding insult to injury. The items in question are:

{Creditor 1 / Account number}

{Creditor 2 / Account number}

{Creditor 3 / Account number}

I find it completely unacceptable that you and the creditor refuse to properly investigate my dispute. Your refusal to follow the Fair Credit Reporting Act is causing me untold stress and anxiety. Since you won't follow through, I want to know exactly how you investigated each account. Therefore, I would like the name, title and contact information for the person at the creditor with whom you did the investigation. This will let me personally follow up with the creditor and find out why they are choosing to report these mistakes on my credit month after month.

I see I am only one person among thousands or more that you have to look after, but to me this is both personally damaging and humiliating. You may not understand it and you don't have to--all I'm asking is that when people look at my credit file, they see the most accurate information and that's not what's happening.

Please provide me with the requested information right away so I can finally put this nightmare behind me.

Looking forward to hear from you as I am actively looking for a new job and wouldn't want these mistakes on my credit report to stand in my way.

Sincerely,

{Your signature}

{Your Printed Name}

{Your Address}

{Your Phone Number}

{Your Social Security Number}

Attach a copy of the credit report showing which accounts you are disputing

Attach a copy of your original letter

Attach a copy of the Bureau's response showing no changes to your credit

Goodwill Letter

A Goodwill letter is a request you make to a creditor based on your past and future relationship. Below is an example of a goodwill letter you can use:

Date:

Name of Credit Bureau

Address of Credit Bureau

City, State, Zip

To Whom It May Concern:

I am writing this letter in hope of getting some assistance with my account number. I am hoping to have an adjustment made out of "Goodwill" on my credit report regarding the late payments that were made on this account. I take full responsibility for my actions. At the time of the late payments I was experiencing a financial hardship and since then I have been consistent with my payment obligations with the company.

I am a loyal satisfied customer with the company and will continue to be long into the future. Based on my past and current payment history it shows that outside of this time period I have always made my payments on time. I would greatly appreciate it if you would consider removing the negative marking that are being report to the credit bureaus. I look forward to hearing back from you as soon as you have made your decision. Thank you so much for your attention to this matter at it is of great importance to me.

Sincerely,

Name:

Address:

Phone number:

If the good will letter fails, then you can try disputing.

Hardship Letter

Think of a hardship letter as an extreme goodwill letter. This letter is used when you have several late payments or are behind on payments and can bring the account current.

In essence, you are asking for a little compassion. Terrible things happen all the time but we all need a break now and again.

Here is a sample letter:

Dear [creditor],

I have recently suffered a serious financial hardship when {spouse died, medical emergency, job loss, business failure, natural disaster... describe the hardship here in moderate detail.}

As a result of this hardship, I have fallen behind on my account with you and would like to do what I can to remedy the situation.

I have {x} late payments on my credit report as a result of this. I am writing to ask, as a matter of good faith, if you would remove the late payments on this account if I can bring the account current and pay all associated late fees.

I would like to salvage my credit and my relationship with you as a creditor as I've been a loyal customer for {x} years!

Any help you can provide or any other options you may have are very much appreciated.

Sincerely,

Customer

While we tend to think of lenders as big uncompassionate machines we need to remember that there are caring and feeling people running those machines.

People can be reasoned with provided you have a real hardship.

Besides, lenders don't make money by sending your account to collections. You just have to give them a reason to work with you and you might be surprised by the results.

Chapter 6. Consequences of Not Paying off Your Debt

What happens when you go into serious delinquency or default on your loans? Well, it depends on the type of loan. With cars and houses, they can be repossessed by the bank. With consumer debt, you are often going to have to declare bankruptcy to wipe out old debts if you are far enough underwater.

Government-backed student loans, however, are a whole different beast. They can NOT be removed via bankruptcy. After 270 days of no payments, they are officially in default and sit there like a bad acne breakout on your credit report, making your score look yucky. Some student loan companies will then turn the loans over to official debt collection companies, which start yammering your phone away about late payments. In addition, you'll be on the hook for their own special fees. Yay.

You might have to try the 'secured credit card' trick to build up your credit again after this kind of financial disaster. Some people want to reach out to a debt settlement company or try to get a payday loan, but please don't! Debt settlement companies have to get paid too, you know, and they'll come after your money one way or another. Most of them are scams. The only honest ones are nonprofits, and even those are doubtful. Payday loans charge sickening interest rates of more than 500% in some cases, so for a $1,000 payday loan, you'll be screwed out of more than $5,000. What kind of sense does that make? Stay far away from them.

If you don't pay your credit cards, they sit untouched with the original creditor for about six months. An original creditor is a bank like Chase, Citi, Capital One, Discover, or American Express. If you keep making payments, even if it's just $10 a month, the account will remain open with the original creditor.

But if you stop making payments for six months, then the original creditor turns the debt along with its collected interest over to a debt collection company. They then attempt to collect the debt for another six months. By now, you've not made a single payment for a year. If no payments are made, then your debt, with any added fees and other expenses from the debt collection company, is then turned over to a law office, where a judgment is brought against you in the form of a lawsuit. The law office represents either the original creditor or the debt buying company. The amount of small claims lawsuits based on collecting past debts has increased significantly in the past ten years, and now there are specialty law firms devoted solely to debt collecting from average people. Well, at least we don't have debtors' prisons anymore.

If this happens, the creditor or debt collector is the plaintiff, and you become the defendant. You can even go to trial and meet with a lawyer to set up court-ordered payment plans based on your actual financial paperwork that you bring to the courthouse. Keep in mind that there is often interest included even after judgment is brought against you.

If you still fail to pay, a lien could be put on your property and your wages could be garnished from your current paycheck. It's legal in most states to garnish up to 25% of your wages. However, if you are seriously buried, you should know that the great state of Texas does not allow wage garnishment so if you are considering a move, Texas might be the place!

Being informed about this entire process will help you make better decisions on repairing your credit before bills go to collections. Dealing with debt collectors is its own game, so let's take a look. It's a bit different than just dealing with a credit card company. The rules have changed.

Make Debt Collectors Go Away

Unfortunately, debt collector companies just won't take your word for it that you're going through a rough time or that they need to leave you alone. They do need to see proof. Collectors love paperwork! The more proof in writing, the better. So, before calling up your debt collector to give them the complete story of why you can't pay, get yourself prepared.

Spend the time gathering up all of your financial paperwork. Get copies of your taxes that show your income and your financial situation. Gather your doctor's bills, your SSDI paperwork, your paystubs, and, if you're sharing an income or living on someone else's SSI, all the paperwork that goes along with that person.

Then, once you've gathered all your paperwork, call up your collector. Keep an eye on the prompts on the phone until you get to the customer service department. Be prepared to wait a long time on the phone. Just set aside the time to devote to this. Be polite, but brief and direct. Tell the representative that you can't pay and you have the proof you can't. Ask them how you can get them the paperwork so they can attach it to your file. Maybe you can send it in an email as a PDF attachment or mail it or fax it to them? Get the name of the representative and the state (or country) where they are. Take down your account number. Ask if you need to provide any other paperwork as proof of the inability to pay. If they tell you that you need something, comply with that. Ask if they can put a financial hardship status on your account. If so, that's great. Many collectors don't.

After you hang up, immediately follow the representative's instructions to send the paperwork to the collector. Keep all originals and only send copies. After two weeks, call up the customer service department again. Explain that you spoke to "Name" and have they received all of your paperwork? Make sure every last piece of paper is attached to your file.

The third step is to put your name on their "Do Not Call" list. VERY IMPORTANT: Keep in mind that they won't call about important stuff, either, like courtesy calls notifying you that your balance has changed. So, do this with caution. Yes, the phone calls are uber annoying. But, that's the primary legal way of contacting you.

You actually need to send your request to not be contacted in writing. Write or type legibly on a blank sheet of paper:

To Capital One,

Please put my name on your "Do Not Call" list. Please remove my name from all call lists. I understand that I will not receive any phone calls.

Thank you,

Your Name

Keep a copy, in case you need it for legal purposes. After you've mailed your request to the collector, wait three weeks for them to receive it and attach the request to your file. Your account will be flagged "Do Not Call" if it's been done properly. Follow up and call the collector to make sure your account has been flagged. Ask the representative if you need to do anything else to make sure you are not contacted.

Throughout this whole negotiating process, continue to send what payments you can. Yes, you can absolutely send small payments to a debt collector, even if it's just $10 or $20 a month. It buys you a little time to change your financial situation. Don't give up and don't just stop sending payments.

You can also settle with debt collectors. Ask them about settlement options and start with less than 50% of the debt owed. They might come back with a counter-offerIf you do this, make sure you have them put Paid in Full on your credit report if possible.

Make sure the proper paperwork is attached to your file and your address is correct. You'd be surprised at how much incorrect information can get attached to your account.

Repair Credit Solution

By making your financial goals, setting your budget, finding ways to save money, and requesting a copy of your credit report, you've done your preliminary legwork in trying to get your finances back in order.

Now that all three credit reporting agencies have a copy of your credit report, it's time to roll up your sleeves and tackle the inaccurate information reported on your credit report.

Reviewing Your Credit Report

When you check each of your credit reports, whether it is on the website of the credit reporting agency where you can download it, or a hard copy of your report which you received in the mail, it is vital that each entry is accurately reported.

When you consider misleading or incorrect information on the credit report, the Equal Credit Reporting Act notes you have the right to dispute the submission with the credit reporting agency. The credit reporting agency has to re-examine the creditor's admission. The enquiry must be concluded within 30 days of receiving the lawsuit message.

If the borrower fails to respond within that time period, the credit reporting agency must delete from the credit report the entry you are contesting. If the creditor replies and the inaccurate entry are corrected, the credit reporting agency will update your credit report. There is also the risk that the borrower can respond to the credit report and not make any changes in it. If you're not happy with your revised credit report, you should write a 100-word paragraph to clarify your side of the story on any of the remaining items on the credit report. This customer statement will then surface any time it appears on your credit report. If you don't want to write a 100-word paragraph on your credit report, you will be able to write another 120-day appeal letter from your most recent credit report.

When you access your credit report on the Website of the credit reporting agency, you will be able to dispute the incorrect entries online. The site will have boxes to check for inaccuracy alongside an appropriate reason. If you choose to write a personalized message, you can also use the same answers as appropriate. Sample answers would be:

- This is not my account.
- This was not late as indicated.
- This was not charged off.
- This was paid off in full as agreed.
- This was not a collection account.
- This is not my bankruptcy as indicated.
- This is not my tax lien as indicated.
- This is not my judgment as indicated.

What you shouldn't do:

- Alter your identity, or try to change it.
- The story is fictional.
- Check any information which is 100% correct.

What you should do:

- Read your emails, should you decide to send them to us? If a letter looks legitimate, credit reporting agencies will believe it has been written by a credit repair service, and they will not investigate the dispute.
- Use your original letterhead (if you do have one).
- Use the appeal form included with the credit report by the credit reporting agency, if you want.
- Provide some evidence suggesting the wrong entry is erroneous.
- Include the identification number for all communications listed on the credit report.

Common Credit Report Errors

Note, there could be various mistakes in each of the three credit reports. It is not uncommon to have positive coverage of an account on one article, but poor reports on another.

Here are some of the most common credit report errors.

- Listed wrong names, emails, or phone numbers.
- Data that refers to another of the same name.
- Duplicate details, whether positive or negative, about the same account.
- Records have negative, apparently positive information.
- Balances on accounts payable are still on view.
- Delinquent payment reports that were never billed in due time.
- This indicates wrong credit limits.
- Claims included in the insolvency which are still due.
- Incorrect activity dates;
- Past-due payments not payable.
- Court records which are falsely connected with you, such as convictions and bankruptcy.

- Tax liens not yours.
- Unprecedented foreclosures.

Spotting Possible Identity Theft

Checking your credit report could also spot potential identity theft. That's why you should inquire at least once a year or every six months for a copy of your credit report.

Things to look for would be:

- Names of accounts and figures that you do not know.
- You don't remember filling out loan applications.
- Addresses you didn't live in.
- Poor bosses or tenants enquiries you don't know.

Creditors Can Help

Many times, if you have had a long-term account with a creditor, you can contact them directly and explain the error being reported on your credit report.

Ask them to write you a letter with the email and correction. Also ask them to contact every credit reporting agency that reports this incorrect entry in order to make the correction.

Once the creditor receives a copy of the letter, make a copy of it and attach the letter to the letter of dispute you send. Mail it to the agency for credit reporting, and ask them to update their files. Once that is completed, you will be sent back a new credit report by the credit reporting agency.

Credit Rescoring

Rapid rescoring is an expedited way of fixing anomalies in the credit file of a customer. The bad news is, you can't do it yourself. A fast rescore dispute process works through borrowers and mortgage brokers, a number of approved registry credit reporting companies, and credit reporting agencies.

If you are a creditor applying for a rescore on your credit report, you would need to provide detailed documents that would be sent to the collateral agencies that are working on your case. Cash registry is the system used by cash grantors. The data archive gathers the records from the three main credit reporting agencies, and has to check the consumer's initial information for a rescore.

Once the verification is entered into the program of the repository a new score will be produced.

The key thing to keep in mind is that a simple rescore can only be temporary. You may be able to close a loan with it, but you must follow through on your credit report with the three main credit reporting firms to ensure it has been removed or corrected. If it reappears, forward the reports immediately to credit reporting agencies.

The downside of a fast rescore is that you save money without having to contend individually with a credit reporting agency that may take longer than 30 days to complete an audit. If the sale of a house or lease depends on your credit score, and you're in a time crunch, the best solution is to easily rescore.

Should You Use a Credit Repair Company?

Using a credit repair company's services is basically hiring a firm to do what you can do for yourself. The process is really without secrets. All the credit repair company does is dispute information on negative entries on your credit report with credit reporting agencies. Most companies may report having agreements with credit reporting agencies or have a secret way to get borrowers to delete unfavorable entries. This is more than likely not true because both state and federal laws under the Fair Credit Reporting Act regulate the credit reporting agencies.

You will be charged a fee for working with a credit repair company. Many systems will call up your credit records or allow you to access your own reports. The letter-writing campaign starts after you have entered into a contract with the firm.

The reason some people hire an outsourced credit repair company is because they feel intimidated or have no time to do the work themselves. Until signing up with a credit repair company there are many steps you need to take. Many businesses operate illegally and you don't want to get caught in that trap.

Beware of Credit Repair Scams

Sadly, it is easy for people to fall prey to credit repair fraud when they are vulnerable and are going through financial challenges. If you're looking for a repair company for cash, here's how to say if it's a genuine or scam business. Many scam firms may only sign up to take the money and run for their services. This is a list of stuff that should raise a red flag.

The company wants you to pay for credit repair services before it provides any services.

- The company doesn't tell you your rights, and you can do it for free. This should appear in any document it presents you with.
- The firm advises that you do not explicitly approach any of the three major national credit reporting agencies. It knows that if you do, you may learn that it took your money, and that it does nothing.
- The company tells you that even if that information is accurate, it can get rid of all the negative credit reports in your credit report. No one can promise just one thing on your credit report for change.
- The company assumes you're trying to create a "different" credit identifier. This is known as file segregation. It is accomplished by filing for the use of an Employer Identification Number to create a new credit report instead of the Social Security number. That is utterly unconstitutional.
- The firm encourages you to challenge any information contained in your credit report regardless of accuracy or timeliness of the material. If the evidence is 100% right, then you have no basis for a disagreement.

Remember, if you are given unlawful advice and follow it knowing it is illegal, you may be committing fraud, and you will find yourself in lawful hot water.

If you use the postal, mobile, or Internet to apply for credit and provide false information, you could be charged and prosecuted with mail or wire fraud. Most of the programs you sign on have a promise that the details you receive are valid when signing the contract.

The Credit Service Organizations Act

Credit repair facilities are governed under State and Federal law by the Credit Service Organizations Act. Under this act, most states require that credit repair companies in each state where they do business be registered and bonded. There are different requirements for each Country. When signing up for this program you will check a copy of your state's Credit Service Organizations Act. The Federal Trade Commission and the offices of the State Attorney General are going after credit repair companies that do not comply with the regulations and are soliciting customers with misleading information. Through visiting: www.ftc.gov, you can also get a copy of the state edition of the Credit Service Organizations Act.

Some of this law's key provisions are for consumer protection by signing up with a credit repair service. A credit repair company must give you a written contract that outlines your rights and obligations that its state has approved. Make sure to read the paperwork before signing something. So know that a credit repair company can't:

- Make false claims about its facilities, before signing.
- Charge yourself until the promised services are complete.
- Provide certain activities until a formal contract has been signed and a three-day waiting period has been fulfilled. You will cancel the contract during this period, without paying any fees.

Chapter 7. How to Proceed with the Letters

Before we get started here, there are a few tips and rules that we need to follow in order to make sure that we are going to get the most out of the templates that we want to use. We are going to take a look at a number of different letters and templates that we are able to send out to the agencies that report our credit so that we can dispute some of the debt or the negative items that are on our reports. These templates will help you compose and keep your dispute as organized as possible. When you pay attention to some of the details that are there, you are going to find that it is easier to come up with a letter that is convincing and effective.

There are a few different ways that we are able to make sure these letters get back to the right parties, and we are going to take a look at all of them below:

Emails

Our world seems to run online all the time and finding ways to work on our credit scores and not have to waste a lot of time copying things or worrying about the paper trails can seem like a great idea. And in some cases, we may find that sending in our 609 letters through email is going to be the best situation for our needs.

Before you do this, though, make sure that you take the time and do the proper research. You want the forms to end up in the right locations, rather than getting sent to the wrong departments, and not doing anything for you in the process. Most of the time there will be listings for the various departments that you want to handle and work with for each credit agency, so take a look at those.

Again, when you are ready, you need to have as many details ready to go for this as possible. Just sending in a few lines about the process and thinking that will get things done is foolish. Write out a letter just like you would if you planned to send these by mail and use that as the main body of your email. Mention Section 609 and some of the disputes that you want to bring up.

In addition to this, you need to take some time adding in the other details. Attach some ways to prove your identity to the email, along with a copy of the credit report that has been highlighted to show what is going on and what you would like to dispute. Add in any of the other documentation that is needed to help support your case, and have it as clean and organized as possible to make sure the right people can find it and will utilize this information to help you out.

Doing it All Online

Many of the credit agencies have made it easier to go through and work on some of these claims online. This helps you out because you will not need to go through and print it all off or worry about finding the paperwork or printing a bunch of things off. And if you are already on your credit report, your identification has been taken care of.

Since so many people are online these days, doing this right from the credit report is a simple and easy process to work with, and you will catch onto it fairly quickly. Do not take the easy way out with this. If you just click on the part that you think is wrong and submit a claim on it, this is not enough. There will not be any reference back to Section 609, and you will not be able to get them to necessarily follow the rules that come with Section 609.

This is where being detailed is going to be useful in the long run. When you do submit one of these claims online, make sure that you write a note with it to talk about Section 609, specifically the part of 609 that you want to reference in this dispute. You can usually attach other forms to document who you are and why you think these need to be dropped.

Treat this just like you would if you tried to mail the information to the credit agency. The more details that you are able to include in this, the better. This will help to build up your case and can make it harder for those items to stay on your credit report for a long period of time. Make sure to mention the 30-day time limit as well.

Telephone

A telephone is one method that you can use, but it is not usually the right one for this kind of process. For example, how easy is it going to be to show the credit agency what your driver's license looks like? You can repeat the number over if you would like, but this process is still a bit more laborious than some of the others and does not always work as well as we would hope it could.

However, this is definitely an option that we can use in order to reach the credit agencies, and for some people who are not sure of what their rights are, or would rather talk directly to the individuals in charge about this issue, the telephone can be the right option. Make sure that you have a copy of your credit report in front of you when you start and having some other identification information and more. There is the possibility that the other side is going to have some questions for you, and they will at least want to go through and verify your identity to make sure they are ready to go. But the same rules apply here, and if you do not get a response within 30 days of that phone call, then the information should be erased.

Keep good records of the conversation, who you talked to during that time, what time and date it was, and so on. This will make it easier to get someone to respond to you and can help us to get this to work in our favor. Also, remember that you will need to repeat these phone calls to all three credit bureaus in order to get your information cleared on all of them.

Mail

Another option that you are able to work with is mail. This is usually a good method to use because it allows you a way to send in all of the information at once. Since you probably already have a physical copy of your SSN, driver's license, the credit report and more, you can get copies of these made pretty quickly, and then send them on with the Section 609 letter that you are working with. This method also allows us a way to go through and circle or highlight the parts of our credit report that we want to point out to the credit reporting agency.

This method is quick and efficient and will make sure that the information gets to the right party. Certified Mail

For the most part, you are going to find that working with certified mail is going to be one of the best options that you can choose. This will ensure that the letter gets to the right place and can tell you for certain when the 30-day countdown is going to begin.

If you send this with regular mail, you have to make some guesses on when the letter will arrive at the end address that you want. And sometimes you will be wrong. If there is a delay in the mailing and it gets there too late, then you may start your 30 days too early. On the other hand, if you assume it is going to take so many days and it takes less, you may wait around too long and miss your chance to take this loophole and use it to your advantage.

Certified mail is able to fix this issue. When the credit agency receives the letter, you will get a receipt about that exact date and even the time. This is going to make it so much easier for you to have exact times, and you can add these to your records. There is no more guessing along the way, and you can be sure that this particular loophole is going to work to your advantage.

Another benefit that comes with certified mail is that you make sure that it gets to its location. If you never get a receipt back or get something back that says the letter was rejected or not left at the right place, then you will know about this ahead of time. On the other hand, if it does get to its location, you will know this and have proof of it.

Sometimes things get lost. If the credit agency says that they did not receive the letter, you will have proof that you sent it and that someone within the business received it and signed for it. Whether the company lost it along the way, or they are trying to be nefarious and not fix the issue for you, the certified mail will help you to get it to all work for you.

When it comes to worrying about those 30 days and how it will affect you, having it all in writing and receipts to show what you have done and when is going to be important. This can take out some of the guesswork in the process and will ensure that you are actually going to get things to work for you if the 30 days have come and gone, and no one will be able to come back and say that you didn't follow the right procedures.

As we can see, there are a few different options that we are able to use when it comes to sending out our Section 609 letters.

Chapter 8. Protect Your Credit: Credit Monitoring

It means monitoring and inspecting your credit history as shown on your credit report. In the end, that is really what it is all about, your credit report and more importantly unexpected changes to your credit report. A credit monitoring service provides this monitoring service for you (for a fee, of course). Most credit monitoring services report that they monitor and track your credit report daily.

What Happens with Credit Monitoring?

When you sign up with a credit monitoring company, they pull all your information from all three credit reporting agencies and typically ask if you are in the process of applying for new credit. Often, they will ask you to check the credit report and verify the information. Of course, they will want to know about any activity you consider suspicious. Now, your new credit monitoring service has a baseline or starting point. Any changes to your credit report going forward could be flagged as possibly fraudulent. Depending on the options available and the monitoring plan you chose, you will be alerted to any suspicious activity that could affect your credit report.

The credit monitoring companies typically are on the alert for:

- New credit inquiries
- Delinquencies
- Negative information that suddenly shows up
- Employment changes
- New credit accounts
- Increased credit lines at existing accounts
- Other changes to your credit report that could be considered a red flag for identity theft

You should note that one reason credit monitoring services have become so popular lately is their alerts for suspicious activity on your credit report is viewed as a counter to identity theft. Some credit monitoring companies even promote their services with this claim.

Advantages

- Constant Tracking - All of your credit reports are constantly tracked. Depending on your choice of credit monitoring companies and plans, this monitoring could be daily or weekly.

- Increased Knowledge - about your own credit. During the time you use a credit monitoring service, you will gain an incredibly valuable firsthand knowledge of how personal credit actually works. Simply by watching the reports provided from your credit monitoring service, you will see in real time how your credit report changes. You will see how even small actions on your part can have a sizeable effect on your credit score. For example, you can watch your credit score drop right after you applied for four different department store credit cards.

- It does not Cost, it saves - Yes, this is a tired old cliché, yet here it truly works. Consider it this way: suppose you use your new knowledge of how your personal credit works, how small things affect your credit score, and that sort of thing to get a better loan rate. Really, it is that easy. For example, let us say you use your newfound credit wisdom to raise your credit score by 75 points.

- Identity Theft Protection - Since your credit report is under constant scrutiny, detection of possible fraudulent activity happens much faster. The credit monitoring service helps you both detect and minimize damage from malicious use of your personal financial information. Additionally, many credit monitoring companies offer legal protections and financial reimbursements. These reimbursements can range from $25,000 to $1,000,000. Surely you have seen the advertisements with the big-name credit monitoring service offering their one-million-dollar guarantee.

- Faster Resolution of Errors - Should you spot an error on one of your many reports sent to you by your credit monitoring service, most of them will assist you in correcting the error.

- No More Guesswork - Since you are paying for professional credit monitoring. Additionally, since your credit monitoring service will alert you for any suspicious activities, you are always aware of what is happening with your credit.

- Less Hassle for You - Yes, credit monitoring can be done yourself as will be explained shortly. However, paying for a credit monitoring service eliminates one more thing for you to do.

Disadvantages

- Price - Of course, all of the services provided by credit monitoring companies comes at a price. Price is one common complaint against credit monitoring companies. Each company sets their own pricing structure. Also, many of them offer different levels of service at different price points.

- Information Disparity - The information available from one credit monitoring service can be vastly different from another credit monitoring service.

- Cancellation Issues - There are various reports (complaints) from past customers of some credit monitoring services regarding the difficulty encountered in cancelling the service.

- Micromanagement Time Wastes - Because your new credit monitoring service provides you with frequent reports and analysis, you may end up trying to micromanage your credit score. This micromanagement could end up costing you a lot of time with few if any substantive changes to your credit score.

- False Sense of Security - Since you are paying for a credit monitoring service, the tendency is to fall into the trap of that is all you need to do to protect yourself. Identity theft protection involves additional areas beyond your credit report that you still need to monitor.

- A Credit Monitoring Service cannot do it as fast as You Might Want - It is not yet possible to monitor a person's credit history on a real time basis. For one thing, many creditors only report information on existing clients weekly or even monthly.

- A Credit Monitoring Service is not the Final Solution - Even the very best credit monitoring service is not capable of fully identifying all fraudulent activity. Consider that there are many credit details that are never even reported to a credit reporting agency.

Chapter 9. Controlling Various Kinds of Debt

Common Types of Debts

It depends on how you choose to see this. There are different kinds or types of debts. We will cut them into four groups to make this fun. Now, the first group.

1. Secured and Unsecured Loans.

Secured loans

Secured loans are the types of debts you get by offering something as surety in case you don't pay that money up. As an example, if you are buying a house, a car, or getting a big work machine, you may opt for a loan when you don't have enough funds to clear the bills yourself. Often, that is a lot of money, and your credit company wants to be sure you're paying it all without complications. So, you are asked to mortgage some of your valued assets in turn. They keep the documents until your payment is complete. If you don't pay up, there are a few legal actions to make, and they sell the assets. The norm is that you take this type of loan on significant assets.

Unsecured loans

Unsecured loans are the direct opposite of secured loans. You do not have to stake anything to access a loan like this. All you need is indicate your interest, submit your essential documents, and the loan is yours. The type of loan you're asking for is what determines what you will be submitting. For example, your credit report may just be enough to get you another credit card. You may have to drop a little deposit plus your credit report when you're signing up for some utilities. All of these have a little or minimal risk by the user. Only that you can cover simple services with this type of loan, no more. Now, you can imagine which weighs higher on a credit score ranked by FICO.

2. Fixed and Revolving Payment Method

Fixed Payment Method

A lot of times, your credit company lays out clear terms, duration, and method of payment to you. When this happens, we say you have got a fixed payment method. Usually, fixed payment methods attract fixed interests too. When you take part in a dealership deal, for example, you may be graced to get that money paid at a particular amount each month and a particular interest rate. Say, the car is worth a thousand USD. You are allowed to pay up in two years, with a total interest of 30%. That is pretty straightforward, right? That's just how fixed payment loans work. A mortgage is an example of fixed payment loans, so you might say they are pretty standard.

Revolving Payment Method:

These types of loans are those that swing like unpredictable bells. There are no exact modalities on most items. You simply take the loans and pay as you can. For example, you can pay when you have the funds; there is no exact deadline for payments. You don't get a limit to interest rates too. Often, your utility, as well as your credit card, fall into this category. This is the exact reason you draw up a credit card, and you can use the credit card as much as you like each month. You don't have to pay up that money when the month ends. You can pay a little now, a lot more over the coming months. But as FICO had earlier advised, it makes perfect sense to draw up only 30% or less of your credit limits. Expectedly, your interest rate is determined by how promptly you clear off that debt.

3. Good and Bad Loans

No questions, this list can't be closed if this group isn't here.

The Good Loans

Classifying loans as good or bad does not exist in official records. Maybe if it did, nobody would ever be excited to try out the bad ones. In any case, a good loan is any loan drawn to invest in resources that may become useful and available over a long period, sometimes, forever. Some of them are:

Mortgage: If it is damning to size up your mortgage and you are planning to hand over the building, my sincere suggestion is that you keep pulling through, and you remain upbeat. This is one of the loans you can't ever regret taking. It is glaring to anyone that houses are assets that you don't use up any moment soon. A house may get into a bad shape sometimes. That's normal. You are expected to keep it brimming with brightness naturally. If you do things right, you can't ever have to pay rents. You also have an asset you can risk to get huge loans to build your career. If things get worse, you can auction the house and restart your careers somewhere. However, you choose to see it, a loan drawn to get a house is a good one. Just be sure you can keep paying till the end before drawing the loan at all.

Student Loans: Well, you might hear someone say drawing student loan in insane. But if you look over the sayings, you'd have something different. You've got to get a good education, and you can't afford it at that moment. It makes perfect sense to tangle yourself in a loan, bag that degree, and pay back much more quickly. As you may fear, your first few years after school would be spent clearing your old debt. But you become free soon, and you'd have access to opportunities you may not have found without top training. From all viewpoints you see this, it is a win-win for all teams. So, I'd vote this as a good loan!

Business: Now, this is another perspective. If you are getting the loans to jack up your investments, you are settling for a good one too. It is undoubtedly a risk, since the business may pick up and may not. But if you probably play your cards right, your business can boom, and that is the start of a goal you didn't see coming.

So, Bad Loans?

Auto loans: For a fact, you must be curious to know why auto loans should be tagged a bad debt, isn't it? I bet!

Well, it is. Auto Loans, dealerships, and whatever kind of car loan you get into is a bad loan. This is because cars are not assets that can be used for a long while. If you sign a two or five-year loan deal, your car is already developing some sorts of problems. So, you'd have to spend on it, and at that same time, pay your auto loans. It would be a mess in a few years.

Credit Card Loans: Credit Card Loans are probably the worst you can take. They can't be used to get important stuff. And either you take note or not, your debt is on the rise with every month you forgot to clear up.

Most Other loans: Most of the other types of loans fall into this category, especially those you draw from friends and family. They are often not precisely significant and should be avoided. Except, of course, they are critical to you, and you are sure there's some way you can quickly pay it all back.

How to Control Your Credit

Regardless of what credit types you have drawn, it is vital to monitor and control it all before it gets out of hand. Even if it's slipped a bit, the best option you've got is to find some way to monitor and control it. Hence, I'll be showing you some easy and practical ways in the next few lines. Here;

1. Don't let things slip off: That's the first rule. Prevention is way better than cure. It stands to reason that if you can plan appropriately and watch out for sinking moments, you shouldn't have to fight to save your credit score fiercely. All you need is to do the math. Where are you heading to? What are your chances of hitting it big or terribly crashing? What would you have to do to avoid falling into a debt pit and struggling to pay up? Several things we might say. Your first job is to find those targets and set them working.
2. Don't spend payments: Pending payments only increase your penalties. Whether for fixed and revolving debts. So, with the facts that you should avoid pending your payments. Clear them off the instant you are able to.
3. Don't toy with revolving debts: Revolving debts are full of surprises. You would usually assume they are the littlest, and so, they can be paid after the much bigger debts. In reality, your revolving debts (like your credit cards) cart

away more than your fixed debts. They tend to increase all the time, and there's a high potential for interest increase too, which doesn't happen in fixed credit cases. Hence, it washes that you should pay them up before considering some other debts at all. Don't delay others too!

If you do the math and your revolving debts are out, you will have a concrete idea of how to tackle the only other debts you have left. This itself is an acute style of controlling debts that you didn't notice. Now you know, cheers.

Chapter 10. Fixing Your Credit Score Fast

Credit bureaus have 30 days to examine complaints and frequently concede to what lenders state about you, regardless of whether it's valid. Regardless of whether all parties concur that a mistake has been made, the errors can continue to manifest in your file on account of the automated idea of most credit reporting. You may need to contact creditors and the bureaus a few times to get mistakes erased. The process may take weeks; best case scenario, you may be taking on the conflict for quite a long time or even years. In case you're amidst attempting to get a mortgage, these errors can cause significant problems. You probably won't have sufficient opportunity to fix your report before the house drops out of escrow or you stall out with an interest rate a lot higher than you have the right to pay.

Issues, for example, these might entice you to turn to one of the numerous organizations that guarantee "moment credit fix" or that assurance to help your credit score. No authentic organization makes such guarantees or certifications, however, so any individual who employs one of these outfits is asking to be misled. There are, in any case, a developing number of certified administrations that can actually fix your credit report errors in 72 hours or less. Read on to learn more.

Fixing Your Credit in a Matter of Hours: Rapid Rescoring

Rapid rescoring administrations came about in light of the fact that such a large number of people were losing loans or paying an excess of interest on account of credit bureau mistakes. Before you get energized, however, you ought to learn what these administrations can and can't do:

- They can't manage you straightforwardly as a consumer—Rapid rescoring is typically offered by little credit-reporting agencies, which fill in as a kind of go between the bureaus and the lending experts. These agencies, which are frequently free, however, which may be auxiliaries of credit bureaus, provide uncommon administrations for loan officials and mortgage representatives, for example, blended or "3-in-1" credit reports. To profit by rapid rescoring, you should work with a loan official or mortgage representative who buys in to an agency that offers the administration.

- They can help you just in the event that you have proof, or if proof can be obtained—Rapid rescoring administrations aren't intended to help people who presently can't seem to begin the credit-fix process. You need something in writing, for example, a letter from the creditor recognizing that your account was reported as late when you were actually reality on time. (This is one reason that it's so necessary to get everything in writing when you're attempting to fix your credit.) If you don't have such proof, however, the creditor has recognized the error, some rapid recorders can get the proof for you. Nonetheless, that may add days or weeks to the process.
- They can assist you with getting errors fixed; however, they can't remove genuine negative things that are in dispute—also, you need proof that a mistake was made—not simply your say as much. If that the credit bureau is already researching your complaint regarding the error, the item typically cannot be included in a rapid rescoring process.
- They can't vow to support your score—"How Credit Scoring Works," sometimes removing negative

items can really hurt a score—strange as that may appear.

The scoring formula attempts to contrast you with people who have comparable credit histories. In the event that you've been lumped into the gathering with a bankruptcy or other dark spots on your report, you may find that your score falls when a portion of those negative items are removed. Rather than being at the highest point of the bankrupts' gathering, as such, you've dropped to the base of the following gathering—the people who have better credit. All the more commonly, removing an error probably won't help your score as much as you may have trusted and probably won't win you a superior interest rate. There are no assurances with rapid rescoring.

Quite a long time ago, brokers and other lending professionals could take care of these problems. In the days prior to the widespread utilization of a credit score, a broker or loan officer could mediate to persuade a lender to disregard mistakes or little imperfections on a client's credit file. Everybody included comprehended that credit report errors were common, and having an accomplished loan pro vouch for your creditworthiness could frequently complete an arrangement.

With the coming of credit scoring and automated loan processes, however, those chances to advocate for clients quickly evaporated. Lending professionals shared consumers' dissatisfaction when incorrect information continued to be reported by the bureaus—information that frequently hosed credit scores and brought about more awful rates and terms than the borrower merited. The mortgage brokers needed an approach to slice through the bureaucracy and accelerate the process. Free credit reporting agencies, with their littler, specific staffs, started to fill the need. Here's the means by which it works. Your broker loan or officer obtains evidence from you that a mistake has been done, and he sends that proof to the credit agency that provides the rapid rescoring service.

The recorders, thusly, have uncommon associations with the credit bureaus that enable their requests to be handled quickly. The rescoring service transfers proof of errors to unique departments at the credit bureaus, and the departments contact the creditors (typically electronically). In the event that the creditor concurs that an error was made, the bureaus quickly update your credit report. After that occurs, another credit score can be calculated. The expense for this service is typically somewhere close to $50 and $100 for each "trade line" or account that is remedied, albeit a few agencies provide the rescoring for no additional charge, as part of a part of services provided to lending professionals.

The presence of rapid rescoring does not change the way that you should be proactive about your credit. Months before applying for any loan, you have to order copies of your reports and start testing any errors. You likewise need to keep your correspondence about these errors. All things considered; rapid recorders typically require some kind of paper trail to pursue to prove to the bureau that the mistakes in fact exist. In any case, If that you wind up highly involved with getting a mortgage and an old problem repeats, rapid rescoring can assist you with disposing of the problem and spare the arrangement.

All in all, how would you discover one of these services? In case you're already managing a loan officer or mortgage broker, ask whether she approaches a rapid rescoring service. If that your lending pro has never known about rapid rescoring—it's an ongoing enough advancement that some haven't—request that her contact the agency that provides her organization with credit reports to check whether it's accessible.

Boosting Your Score in 30 to 60 Days

Rebuilding your credit can sometimes be an excruciatingly slow process, yet you can take a couple of easy routes that may increase your score in as meager as a month or two, as talked about in the accompanying segments.

Pay Off Your Lines of Credit & Credit Cards.

Probably the fastest approaches to support a score is to lower your debt use proportion—the distinction between the amounts of revolving credit that is accessible to you and the amount that you're utilizing. One straightforward approach to improve your proportion is to redistribute your debt. In the event that you have a big balance on one card, for instance, you could transfer probably a portion of the debt to different cards. It's usually better for your scores to have little balances on a number of cards than a big balance on a solitary card. You additionally could explore getting a personal installment loan with your nearby credit association or bank, and utilize the cash to pay down your cards. Applying for the loan may affect your scores a piece; however, that is probably going to be more than offset by the development to your scores from lessening the balances on your credit cards. (Credit scoring formulas are substantially more delicate to the balances on revolving debt, for example, credit cards, than to the balances on installment loans.)

Utilize Your Credit Cards Lightly

A big difference between your balances and your limits is what the scoring formula likes to see —and it doesn't really care whether you pay off your balances in full each month or carry them from month to month. What makes a difference is the amount of your credit limits you're really utilizing at some random time. A few people demand they've supported their scores by paying off their cards in full a couple of days before their announcement closes. In the event that their credit card backers, as a rule, send out bills around the 25th, for instance, these people check their balances online about seven days prior and pay off whatever's owed, in addition to a couple of bucks to cover any charges that may manifest before the 25th. When the bills are really printed, their balances are pretty close to zero. (In the event that you utilize this method, simply make sure you make a second payment after your announcement shows up if your balance isn't already zero. That will make sure you don't get damaged with late charges—and truly, that can occur, despite the fact that you made a payment before in the month.)

Concentrate on Correcting the Big Mistakes on Your Credit Reports

If that another person's bankruptcy, collections, or charge-offs are showing up on your report, you will probably profit by having those removed. If that an account you closed is reported as open, then again, you'll probably need to disregard it. Having an account filed as "closed" on your file can't support your score and may hurt it.

Utilize the Bureaus' Online Dispute Process

Some credit-fix veterans swear they get faster results along these lines, however regardless, you'll have to make printouts of all that you send to the bureaus and each correspondence you get from them.

Check whether You Can Have Your Creditors Update Positive Accounts or to Report

Not all creditors report to every one of the three bureaus, and some don't report reliably. If that you can get a creditor to report an account that is in good standing; however, you may see a quick knock in your score.

Chapter 11. Little Known Facts about Credit

Credit Cards Secrets Revealed

The first step when applying for a credit card is knowing the actual purpose why you are choosing to apply for a credit card in the first place. Some people find credit cards with cash reward to be very attractive. While other people may want to apply for a credit card offering a 12 to 18-month intro of 0% interest rate, so they can make purchases without paying interest for a specific time and take advantage of balance transfers. There are many more reasons why consumers apply for credit cards, but it is important to know the ins and outs about credit card so you can make well-informed decisions.

One of the most important things a consumer should know before applying for a credit card is their credit score. Consumers with excellent credit usually qualify for the best offers, but having average to poor credit often means a consumer will pay higher interest rates and possibly hefty annual fees.

Understanding Interest Rates

So, you recently applied for a credit card offering 0% for 6months, fast forward two weeks later you checked your mail and there it is your brand-new credit card with a

$5000 limit. You are thrilled because you were planning on using the credit card to book a trip to Cancun and pay off the card over the next five months. So you wasted no time to book your ticket and hotel room; you also purchased things you think are necessary for your trips such as new clothes and shoes. Before long your credit card balance jumped up to $4,500, but not to worry about now because you are planning on paying off your debt before the six-month intro zero per cent grace period expires. Unfortunately, you were not able to pay off your credit card before the six-month interest grace period. To make matters worse, you were only making a minimum payment of approximately $105 every month. But six months later your minimum payments were being applied to the interest and principal on your credit card balance, instead of being applied to just the principal balance. Therefore, if you were to keep making the minimum payment of $105 it would have taken you 56 months to pay off the credit card. You would have also paid approximately $1,280 in interest payments.

Annual Percentage Rate

When you initially applied for a credit card your annual percentage rate (APR) was 11.24%. However, what does this all mean to you? The APR is the annual cost of borrowing money from your credit card. The APR specifically applies to the interest rate that will be charged, if your credit card balance is not paid in full on or before the due date.

Types of APR

There are usually several types of APR that applies to your credit card account. For example, there is an APR for purchases. There is an APR for cash advance, balance transfers; there is an APR that usually goes into effect when you make a late payment or if you violate any other terms of your credit card agreement.

Can My Credit Card Rate Increase?

Your credit card rate can increase if a promotional rate has expired, your credit card rate can increase when you don't follow your credit card terms, when changes are made to a debt management plan and if your variable rate increases. What exactly is a debt management plan?

A debt management plan is an official agreement between a creditor and a debtor pertaining to a debt owed to the creditor by the debtor. The program is also designed to help the borrower pay off his or her outstanding debt faster. A debt management plan or debt relief plan is often a service a third party company offers to someone who cannot afford to pay their debts on unsecured accounts. The third-party company (debt Relief Company) will collect the payment from the debtor and then distribute it to the creditor. A debtor often uses a debt relief company, because the company may help them to evaluate their debt, help the debtor to come up with a budget, establish a time frame to pay off their debt and negotiate with creditors on their behalf.

A debtor usually enters into a debt management plan with a creditor when they are facing some financial hardship that makes it difficult for them to make even the minimum payments on their loan or credit card. The debt management plan will most likely include an agreement to allow the debtor to make an affordable payment to the creditor. The creditor will probably agree to dramatically reduce the interest rate on the debtor balance or outright eliminate the interest on the debtor balance.

Credit Bureaus

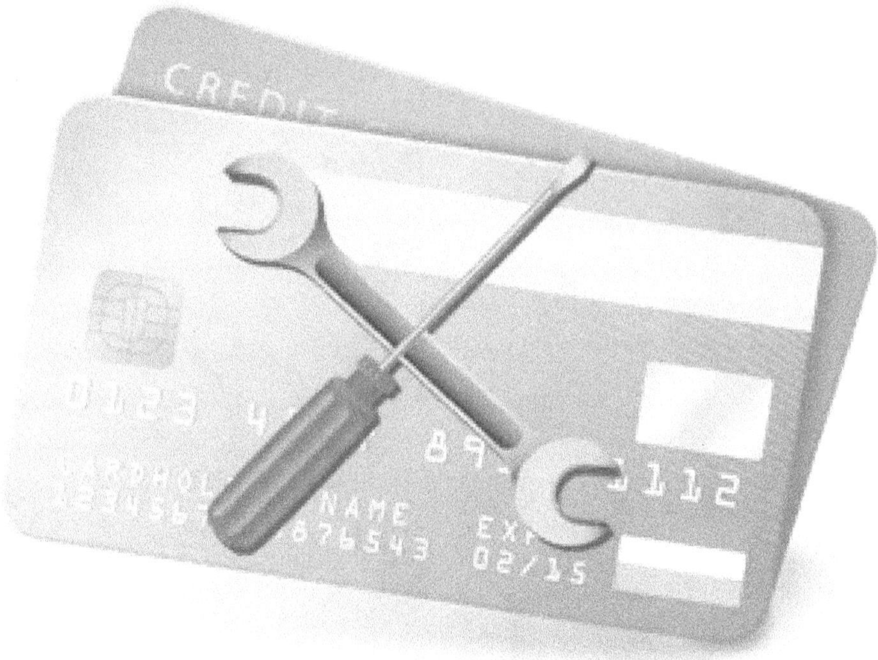

Credit bureaus are privately held, billion-dollar organizations whose primary reason for existing is to make cash; that is what revenue driven organizations do right? They keep data that lenders furnish them - regardless of whether accurate or inaccurate - about our credit association with them and sell it. This straightforward plan of action generates over $4 Billion per year!

One wellspring of income for them originates from selling the information on our credit reports to different lenders, managers, insurance agencies, credit card organizations - and whoever else you approve to see your credit information. In addition to the fact that they provide them with crude data; yet they likewise sell them various methods for examining the data to decide the risk of stretching out credit to us. In addition to trading our information to lenders, they likewise sell our information to us - credit scores, credit observing administrations, extortion security, wholesale fraud prevention - interestingly enough this region has quickly gotten perhaps the greatest wellspring of income. Furthermore, those pre-endorsed offers in our letter drop each week; or garbage mail? That's right; they got our information from the credit bureaus as well. Organizations buy in to an assistance provided by the three credit bureaus that sell them a rundown of consumer's credit information that fit a pre-decided criterion.

Presently, as opposed to prevalent thinking, credit bureaus don't have any contribution on whether you ought to be endorsed for a loan or not; that is absolutely based on the credit criteria of the lender you're working with. However, by utilizing the entirety of the information that has been set on your credit report (personal information, payment history, and credit propensities) and FICO's technique for scoring that data, they do tell them with how creditworthy you are.

Origin and History of Credit Bureau

In recent decades, credit has gotten easier and easier to obtain. Credit cards, for example, were once given to the wealthier classes in the public eye and were utilized just occasionally. Toward the start of the twenty-first century, practically 50% of all Americans had in any event one broadly useful credit card (that is, a Visa, MasterCard, American Express, or Discover card). The ascent of credit as a typical method to buy necessities, extravagances, and everything in the middle of implies that credit bureaus process more information and are a more crucial part of the general economy than any other time in recent memory. Credit bureaus likewise monitor and investigate the data got from a regularly expanding number of loans for homes, cars, and other high-cost things.

Today, credit bureaus consistently accumulate information from creditors (banks; credit-card guarantors; mortgage organizations, which have practical experience in loaning cash to home buyers; and different businesses that stretch out credit to people and businesses) and amass it into files on singular consumers and businesses, while refreshing their current files. In addition to the data gathered from creditors, credit files may likewise contain one's business history, previous addresses, false names, bankruptcy filings, and removals. Information usually remains on a credit report for seven years before being evacuated.

The greater part of the nearby and provincial consumer credit bureaus in the United States are claimed by or are under agreement to one of the three essential consumer credit-reporting administrations referenced previously. Every one of these three organizations assembles and appropriates information separately, and credit scores and reports vary somewhat from bureau to bureau. Each organization keeps up around 200 million singular consumer credit files. Frequently a lender will utilize an average of the credit evaluations provided by the three unique bureaus when choosing whether to make a loan.

The basic business credit bureau in the United States is Dun and Bradstreet. D and B have credit files on more than 23 million associations in North America and on more than 100 million businesses around the globe. In addition to giving creditors information important to decide a credit applicant's capabilities, credit bureaus make their data accessible for progressively questionable purposes. For example, standard mail advertisers regularly buy information from credit bureaus as they continued looking for potential clients. If that you have ever gotten a letter revealing to you that you have been pre-endorsed for a particular credit card at a particular yearly percentage rate, it is valid; the credit-card organization definitely realizes your credit rating and has to be sure previously affirmed you for the predefined card. Forthcoming managers and proprietors sometimes buy credit histories, as well.

What Credit Bureaus Do?

Credit bureaus collect information from various sources in accordance with consumer information. The activity is done for various reasons and includes data from singular consumers. Included is the information concerning a people charge payments and their getting. Utilized for evaluating creditworthiness, the information provides lenders with an outline of your accounts if a loan repayment is required. The interest rates charged on a loan are additionally worked out concerning the kind of credit score shown by your experience. It is thusly not a uniform procedure, and your credit report is the significant instrument that affects future loans.

Based on risk based valuing, it pegs various risks on the various customers in this manner deciding the cost you will acquire as a borrower. Done as credit rating, it is an assistance provided to various interested parties in the public. Terrible credit histories are affected for the most part by settled court commitments that mark you for high interest rates every year. Duty liens and bankruptcies, for example, shut you out of the conventional credit lines and may require a great deal of arrangement for any loan to be offered by the bank.

Bureaus collect and examine credit information including financial data, personal information, and elective data. This is given by various sources generally marked data furnishers. These have an exceptional association with the credit bureaus. An average gathering of data furnishers would comprise of creditors, lenders, utilities, and debt collection agencies. Any association that has had payment involvement in the consumer is qualified including courts. Any data collected for this situation is provided to the credit bureaus for grouping. When it is accumulated, the data is placed into specific repositories and files claimed by the bureau. The information is made accessible to customers upon request. The idea of such information is important to lenders and managers.

The information is in this manner material in various conditions; credit evaluation and business thought are simply part of these. The consumer may likewise require the information to check their individual score and the home proprietor may need to check their inhabitants report before renting an apartment. Since borrowers saturate the market, the scores will, in general, be robotic. Straightforward examination would deal with this by giving the client a calculation for speedy appraisal. Checking your score once every other year should deal with errors in your report.

Individuals from the public are qualified for one free credit report from every one of the significant bureaus. Business reports, for example, Paydex might be gotten to on request and are chargeable. Lawful expressions for the credit bureaus incorporate credit report agency, CRA in the US. This is organized in the Fair Credit Report Act, FCTA. Other government rules associated with the assurance of the consumer incorporate Fair and Accurate

Credit Transaction Act, Fair Credit Billing Act and Regulation B. Statutory bodies have additionally been made for the regulation of the credit bureaus. The Fair Trade Commission serves to as a controller for the consumer credit report agencies while the Office of the Comptroller of Currency fills in as a manager of all banks going about as furnishers.

Transunion, Equifax and Experian

Three Major Credit Bureaus

The popular credit bureaus have a significant effect on every consumer, but many people don't know these companies or how they work.

- Experian
- Equifax
- Trans Union

The ideal approach to manage your credit capably and assume responsibility for your financial circumstance is to be educated. This takes a brief period and exertion on your part, yet since your credit scores are so important to dealing with your accounts and setting aside cash, it's your duty to know as much as you can regard the credit bureaus that formulate credit appraisals. To assist you with getting a running beginning on that strategy, some information on Transunion, Experian and Equifax, the primary credit bureaus in the U.S.:

Transunion

Transunion has workplaces the nation over that manages various parts of credit: credit management, identity theft, and other credit issues; and types of credit customers, for example, personal, business, and press inquiries. If you discover errors on your Transunion credit report, you can call them at 800.916.8800 or visit their site to debate them. If that you believe that you're a casualty of identity theft, call them at 800.680.7289 at the earliest opportunity.

Experian

Like other credit bureaus, Experian provides a wide range of various administrations for people, businesses, and the media rather, they encourage guests to utilize online forms for questions, identity theft reports, and different issues.

Equifax

Based in Atlanta, GA, Equifax likewise has various departments to help people with various types of questions and concerns. Their website is additionally set up to have people utilized online forms to address errors, report identity theft, and handle different concerns. In any case, if somebody believes that their identity has been taken, the individual in question can, however, call 888.397.3742 to report it to Equifax. If that somebody detects a blunder on their Equifax credit report, that person must utilize the contact number on the report to question it. There is no number on the site to describe errors.

These are the 3 credit bureaus in the nation, and they each adopt an alternate strategy to enabling people to get in touch with them to pose inquiries or address any issues they might be encountering. Rather than reaching the credit bureaus legitimately, numerous people prefer to utilize a credit checking administration to assist them with dealing with their credit and stay over their funds. The credit bureaus all have comparative projects; however, most people prefer to utilize a free organization to assist them with these issues. That way, they get an impartial perspective on their credit score and a lot more devices to proactively manage and improve their credit ratings.

These companies have a great history in the financial industry. Also known as a credit reporting agency, it gathers financial information about consumers and combines this information into a single report. Since these bureaus work independently, the credit report that a single bureau generates for an individual could be slightly different from another bureau's report. Although there are smaller credit bureaus, the top three serve a more significant share of the market.

The credit bureaus have a fascinating profit model. Lenders, banks, and many other companies share a lot of information about their clients with credit bureaus for free. The credit bureaus process this information and put it on sale, in the form of a credit report, to different parties that require insight into your financial history, and more.

Thinking about just one number to represent your credit score is a little too simple. You actually have multiple credit scores, each calculated and maintained by a different company. Usually these scores are very close to each other, but they almost always vary by at least a few points.

The three bureaus are Equifax, Experian, and Transunion. We will get into the reason that the scores are different a little bit later, but it has to do with the way they collect information. Your score from any of these three companies will be called your FICO.../../Downloads/h - _ftn1 score (it may also be a BEACON score from Equifax). If it is called something different, it is just an estimate, and is not the real deal.

As we will find out later, that may be ok in some cases, but it is something you should be aware of.

In addition to the three companies, each one actually keeps up to 7 different scores per person. For our purposes, we are just going to focus on what is called the classic or generic score. So from here on out, the words "score" or "credit score" mean the classic or generic score. It is the most commonly used for most purposes (buying a house or getting a loan), and the other scores will follow it up or down for the most part. We aren't worried about two or three points here, we are looking for the biggest changes we can make with the least effort.

Dealing with Credit Bureaus

Today, where the economy is at its weak point, having a good credit is a necessary tool. This is because it allows you to obtain house loans, car loans, credit card, and other convenient financial services and instruments. You may be able to live without having a good credit.

You can discern the credit bureau that holds your file by looking at any rejection letter you received from a recent credit application.

If you are dealing with the credit bureau that handles your file, keep in mind that it belongs in the business of collecting and selling information. As such, you should not provide them with any detail, which is not necessary legally.

When you already have your credit report, make sure to check for any error or discrepancy. If you find anything that is questionable in your report, you can send the credit bureau a written request for them to investigate on the error. In general, the credit bureau has the burden of documenting anything that is included in your credit report. If the credit bureau fails to investigate on the error or neglects your request for an investigation within 30 days, the error should be removed.

You need to educate yourself about the legal obligations of credit bureaus in order to have a successful credit repair process. Prior to dealing with them, make sure you know all the legal aspects so you would not end up paying for something that should not be charged with a fee. Remember, credit bureaus are also businesses and that they own many credit repair companies.

Making the Best of Credit Bureaus

It is a little annoying to learn that all three credit bureaus have sensitive financial data. However, there's no method to prevent lenders and collection entities from sharing your information with the above companies.

You can limit any possible problems associated with the credit bureaus by evaluating your credit reports annually, and acting immediately in case, you notice some errors. It is also good to monitor your credit cards and other open credit products to ensure that no one is misusing the accounts. If you have a card that you don't often use, sign up for alerts on that card so that you get notified if any transactions happen, and regularly review statements for your active cards. Next, if you notice any signs of fraud or theft, you can choose to place a credit freeze with the three credit bureaus and be diligent in tracking the activity of your credit card in the future.

How the Bureaus Get Their Information

To learn how the score is calculated, first we need to learn about all the different inputs of your score, aka where the bureaus get their info. You may have many factors that report information to the credit bureaus, or none.

Credit cards are called revolving accounts or revolving debt by the credit bureaus. Each monthly payment and balance is reported, as well as any late payments. This means that any cards that have your name on them will also report to all the bureaus. This includes cards that belong to a spouse or parent. If you're an authorized user on the account it gets reported on your credit no matter what. Many people have their credit ruined by a spouse or parent going into bankruptcy or not paying their credit card bills. If your name is on any credit cards that belong to people that may not pay their bills, ask them to take your name off immediately!

Installment loans also report information to the credit bureaus. If you went down to your local Sears and financed a washer/dryer set by putting up a down payment, that is an installment loan. The details of these loans are all reported; the total balance, as well as the timeliness and amounts of your monthly payments.

If you have mortgages or student loans, that information does get reported. Total amounts due, total paid so far, and the status of monthly payments is all reported. This information is all kept track of and organized in their databases.

Conclusion

If you want to repair your credit then here are some steps that might be more effective. The first step is to gather your finances together and make a budget. Sometimes the problem isn't about paying what you owe so much as it is about priorities. Next, save up an emergency fund of at least $1000 in case of any unexpected expenses that pop up in the future. Next, tackle the collection agencies. Many of them will work with you if you explain your situation, and are willing to pay less than the full amount if you can afford it. It might be worth looking into a credit counselor as sometimes they can help with creditors and make things easier on your financial situation.

Credit repair service is a process that creates an accurate financial history for a customer and helps to increase their credit score. One of the ways in which your credit score can be increased is by obtaining new loans, paying off old loans, and making payments on time. A good credit score will give you access to better interest rates as well as other financial services.

Your credit score will be scarred regardless if they fix it or not. And, because the credit repair company is charging you a fee to fix your score, the chances are that you will have to pay for their services in the future. There are many websites out there that will list top credit repair companies, and while some of them work, some of them are just trying to get your money. In addition, some people think the credit repair companies are legitimate and then end up paying for their services anyways. It is the easiest solution because you can pick up phone calls from these companies, but be careful. You have to make sure that you do not give any personal contact information to these credit repair companies because they are fakes. If you want to use a credit repair company, do some research on your own before you give them any personal Information? If you are not sure about the credit repair company, then you can go to the Better Business Bureau and see how many complaints they have. Also, check the state department's website for complaints against the company. If there are hundreds of complaints that they are a scamming company then do not give them any money. Trust me, it is better to be safe than sorry.

You may be in denial about the state of your credit, but if you are planning on applying for any loans or credit cards, it is imperative that you try and fix. Nowadays people rely on their credit scores more than ever before to determine their eligibility for loans and other types of credit. Such companies are highly skilled in the art of repairing credit, and can help you avoid some of the most common pitfalls. If you have suffered a serious hit to your score due to late payments or bankruptcies, it could take years before your score is restored to its former glory. That's because it takes time for your creditors to update their records with your current status, you should pay off any outstanding debts and make your payments on time. If you have made a few late payments recently, or have otherwise damaged your credit score, contact the creditor or consumer reporting agency. Explain that you have had some trouble recently, but you are now working to rectify the situation and would like to make a payment arrangement. Many creditors and agencies will work with consumers who show a sincere desire to repay their debts.

Finally, my opinion on the best way to improve your credit is to make a budget for yourself and stick to it! If you can avoid doing that, then your credit will be in great shape.